Smart Net

Smart Net

From Inert Data to Sentient Life

Steven H. Kim

Writer's Showcase
San Jose New York Lincoln Shanghai

Smart Net
From Inert Data to Sentient Life

All Rights Reserved © 2002 by Steven H. Kim

Writer's Showcase
an imprint of iUniverse, Inc.

For information address:
iUniverse, Inc.
5220 S. 16th St., Suite 200
Lincoln, NE 68512
www.iuniverse.com

ISBN: 0-595-21382-0

Printed in the United States of America

For Eunho Lee and the surfers

Contents

Preface

With the turn of the millennium, zippy advances in information technology and its applications have swept away traditional assumptions regarding information access, knowledge acquisition, and group interaction. Life at work, study and play is undergoing a radical transformation which renders obsolete large swathes of time-honored practices. In the popular press, the new order has been proclaimed a second industrial revolution.

This fertile soil has engendered a rich crop of books and articles over the years. The harvest of literature has covered a large variety of digital techniques and novel practices.

The publications tend to be of two types. The first is the technical sort, which offers a mass of information for specialists in the field. The drawback is that the material is inscrutable to most outsiders who require an orientation to the Net and its implications.

The second type of literature offers a charming enumeration of case studies in education, marketing, logistics, or some other subject. Unfortunately, these tracts are specialized in their own way and fail to provide a panoramic view of the digital world. Moreover, books of this kind largely ignore the history and technology behind the innovations. Without a holistic view of the past and present, only a witch doctor would feel confident about envisaging the future.

Despite the wealth of information - or perhaps because of it - there has been a dearth of organizing frameworks for grasping the myriad tools, techniques, and strategies for cyberspace. This small volume is intended to help fill the gap. It strives to present a balanced perspective, to filter the melody from the noise, and to offer a sense of coming attractions.

The book presents a survey of Internet technologies and their applications. It describes the rise of the Net from its halting origins in the 1960s to its gradual transformation into an icon of the informatic society. The topics on display range from historical milestones and software concepts to online products and managerial strategies.

The Internet is a universal platform for boosting the productivity of the individual and for enhancing the competitiveness of the enterprise. The primer begins with an introduction to the core technologies as well as macrolevel trends. This is followed by a set of frameworks for analyzing the environment, developing a holistic strategy, and preparing for the future. The discussion covers the gamut of applications at the office, school, and home.

The last chapter explores a variety of emerging directions for the Web. The Net has already established itself as an indispensable part of a knowledge-based society. Today it is a boundless medium to support life in a digital world. Tomorrow it will turn into a haven for synthetic minds and a nexus for all life in this corner of the universe.

The material in this book has grown from a series of lectures to a diverse set of audiences in both industry and academe. On various occasions, the participants from industry have ranged from entry-level employees to venture capitalists and top executives of global corporations. The academic audience has spanned the entire campus, from first-year undergraduates to doctoral candidates and seasoned researchers in sundry disciplines. Most participants had scant experience with computers or their applications, and desired a coherent introduction to the field.

Thanks to these kaleidoscopic origins, the volume should be of interest to many readers, ranging from front-line workers to senior executives as well as students of all ages. Given the breadth of coverage in this book, one reader is likely to take a special interest in one string of chapters plus appendices, and another person in a different chain.

The volume may be used for self-study or as a group text. In the latter case, the book can serve as a primary reference for a professional workshop on the basics of the Internet, online media, virtual products, or digital commerce. Another setting takes the form of academic courses in a variety of disciplines relating to computer applications, technical trends, electronic commerce, or corporate strategy.

Whatever the venue, the handbook presents a compact survey of online concepts and technologies, as well as their deployment for competitive advantage. In sum, the volume can serve as a systematic guide to emerging trends for the general reader, or as a tool for strategic planning for the decision maker.

It has taken several years of writing and testing to fashion a book on the Internet for a diverse audience. If the reader comes to borrow from its pages on occasion while preparing for the future, then that would be my rich reward.

S. K.

Chapter 1

Digital Planet

As the millennium dawns, the information revolution is transforming the world at an unprecedented rate. Digital technologies have been advancing at a furious clip since the middle of the 20th century. Leaps in processing power, transmission media, and storage capacity have enhanced the speed of computation, spread of information, and ease of communication. Moreover, the windfall has occurred in parallel with a plunge in cost.

Around the world today, children play games in virtual worlds while students write reports using online data and homemakers retrieve recipes via the Web. Meanwhile, managers procure business intelligence on the Net while engineers collaborate on projects across gaps in time and space. The digital medium is a vehicle for capturing data, conveying knowledge, and even expressing emotion.

The advent of the Web has brought an era of lively and timely content fortified with multimedia features. A compelling mode of participation lies in virtual reality, which allows for an immersive experience in a simulated world with the freedom to roam in three spatial dimensions. Cyberspace can merge images, video, animation, and text to provide an engrossing environment. The sparkle of dynamic media in concert with the active involvement of the user makes the customized experience more intense, enjoyable, and memorable.

Another development in its infancy lies in smart programs which can automatically extract useful knowledge from a mishmash of data. Clever software can also tailor a presentation to the user's needs of the moment as well as his general level of knowledge.

Promises and Threats

When deployed sensibly, information technology is a powerful platform for boosting both efficiency and effectiveness for an individual or an organization. As a case in point, many people today rely so much on their email that their productivity would plummet without it. In a similar way, most organizations in a modern economy would practically grind to a halt with a breakdown in their internal networks. The same is true for the loss of digital lifelines to suppliers, customers, and other stakeholders.

Yet it was not always thus. For three decades starting in the 1960s, organizations around the world had invested heavily in information technology. The expenditures were driven by a conviction that the new techniques would raise productivity and enhance the quality of products and services.

Unfortunately, both personal experience and collective studies usually failed to detect any increase in the productivity of the enterprise. Apparently, the savings due to the automation of transactions were offset by the costs of implementing the platform.

Another stumbling block lay in the clumsy use of the system. An informatic package could swiftly accumulate a mountain of facts. But the data would often remain closeted in massive databases, untouched by overworked analysts. It was difficult to find an organization which could absorb the mounds of data or to convert them into useful knowledge.

Another challenge lay in the soaring pace of business activity. Rapid changes in the world outside required a constant evolution of information systems to access and analyze facts in inventive ways. These demands were accompanied by a proliferation of modes for digital information: not only numerical data, but voice, fax, video, hypertext and multimedia.

The clunky tools available for development also ensured slow progress in building mission-critical systems. Major applications would take years to complete, by which time the functional requirements had changed in response to environmental shifts, organizational restructuring, product renovation, and employee transfers. Against the advance of digital technologies as well as the press of secular trends such as globalization, a newly-minted system would often be obsolete upon completion and sometimes even earlier.

To the surprise of many observers, however, the promise of informatics began to be fulfilled during the 1990s. By this juncture, a number of tools had arrived on the scene to help manage the ocean of data in meaningful ways. The advances lay in open standards for presenting and conveying data as well as techniques for synthesizing knowledge from inert data.

For the most part, the crucial technologies have taken the form of software rather than hardware. One of the vanguards of the digital revolution is found in Internet standards for online communication. A versatile platform within the Net lies in the World Wide Web for accessing information anywhere on the global network. An attendant feature is the ease of producing and viewing multimedia content in formats ranging from text and sound to animation and video.

For organizations around the globe, the confluence of Internet protocols, Web standards, and related technologies has been a godsend. One consequence takes the form of the *intranet.* As a synthesis of open standards and multimedia features, an intranet is a convenient platform for developing information systems and disseminating information throughout an enterprise.

An intranet may be extended beyond the walls of an organization to include other actors, including suppliers and customers. An *extranet* brings the benefits of an intranet to the entire supply chain – from component suppliers to ultimate consumers – as well as other stakeholders such as alliance partners.

Atop the networking and formatting schemes for locating, conveying, and presenting information are intelligent tools to support knowledge level work. Software *agents* can serve as guides to help novices with simple tasks or to aid experts with abstruse goals. The tools of *data mining* can discover knowledge from raw facts, even when subtle patterns lay camouflaged within sprawling datasets contaminated by noise.

The "new" technologies have a long lineage. For instance, the Internet protocol that underlies an extranet was born of visionary projects sponsored by the U.S. Department of Defense in the mid-1960s. To cite another example, a foundation for data mining lies in the panoply of schemes from artificial intelligence, a discipline whose awkward name dates back to a seminal conference in 1956.

These new/old techniques are transforming commercial and non-profit organizations in a dramatic way. When wielded with skill, the tools produce solid benefits on the bottom line. For instance, data mining programs have reportedly yielded returns on investment of 300 percent or more for some applications; in other terms, a dollar invested today would produce three dollars' worth of benefits a year down the road. Moreover, the return on investment for intranets have at times surpassed an astounding 1,000 percent.

Tidal Waves

The Internet has begun to rework the fabric of society, from the living room and classroom to the boardroom and playroom. One way to categorize the impact of the information highway lies along the dimensions of flexibility, speed, and cost.

The Net offers voluminous information at the fingertips. The commercial benefits of digitopia have already been mentioned. For the consumer, the Web provides a convenient tableau for comparing the features, prices and terms of sale among similar products. Software agents can swiftly compare related offerings, while displeased consumers can easily switch vendors with the click of a mouse. One outcome of the freewheeling range of choices is a shift of power from the seller to the buyer.

A second consequence of cyberspace is an increase in the tempo of transactions. For instance, a request for information can be transmitted, processed, and fulfilled at once. What used to take days or weeks through traditional channels is likely to run its course within seconds on the Net. The result is an acceleration in the pace of personal interaction as well as business activity.

The Internet is also a platform for reducing transaction costs. For instance, a transfer of funds from a bank account costs less than 1 cent on the Net, versus 27 cents at an automated teller machine, or 52 cents over the phone. In the travel industry, processing an airline ticket via the Web costs $1, versus $8 on average by a human travel agent.[1] The increase in efficiency leads to an expansion in the number of transactions for all activities, thereby enhancing personal satisfaction as well as fueling economic growth in general.

The changes sweeping around the globe reflect only the wavefront of a virtual tsunami. To date the Internet has barely begun to affect daily life and routine commerce.

In the realm of leisure, multimedia technics have established a beachhead in the cinemas and playrooms of the world. Their impact can be seen through special effects in feature films and game consoles. At the dawn of the 21st century, integrated media began to infuse prosaic applications by way of digital video on mobile phones, vocal commands on personal organizers, and real-time conferencing on wide area networks.

A third set of capabilities which will revolutionize life to a greater extent than the Internet itself lies in brainy software. Since the early 90s, leading enterprises have deployed autonomous programs to pry fresh knowledge from canned data. Applications of the technology range from predicting user preferences to forecasting financial markets and piloting autonomous vehicles.

In recent years, self-learning schemes such as neural networks have begun to appear in consumer products, as exemplified by toy pets with personality. The wares on offer, however, represent only the first generation of applications.

The full force of learning software will not be felt until they power truly smart agents for boosting personal productivity. The applications include virtual butlers to handle simple queries from online visitors as well as travel mates to translate among several languages. Other examples of clever agents encompass ever-alert aides to distill the news, or alter egos to respond to messages while their owners are engaged at work or play.

Road to Cyberia

The first pebbles on the road to cyberia were laid in the misty haze of antiquity. Advances in mathematics and computation occurred in fits and starts over the millennia, taking two steps forward and one or two backward. What one culture laid in stone, a marauder might misplace or even willfully destroy.

The ambling path to digitopia turned into a direct road only in modern times. It seems ironic that the seeds of economic growth and global communication were sown in the midst of war, one hot and the other cold. On the other hand, if we recognize war as a wellspring of innovation, the outcome is not as remarkable.

By the beginning of the 20th century, a number of mechanized tools for computation had been constructed for specific tasks. An example lay in the tabulating devices used to analyze census data in the United States.

Rapid advances in computation occurred during the Second World War. One fertile ground for innovation lay in intelligence services. A few years before the outbreak of hostilities, the German military had constructed a mechanical device called the Enigma. The machine was used during the war to encrypt directives from Nazi headquarters to units in the field.

Fortunately for the Allied effort, British intelligence devised a countermeasure known as the Ultra system to decode enemy transmissions. The latter contraption alerted the Allies to impending movements of the enemy and thereby played a pivotal role in winning the war.

The development of the computer continued apace after the cessation of hostilities. In time, electromechanical devices such as the vacuum tube came to usurp the role of mechanical components and helped to usher in the age of the modern computer.

A conceptual breakthrough was achieved by the mathematician John von Neumann, an American of Hungarian descent. His idea involved the unification of instructions and data. If commands were viewed as flexible input much like numerical data, then a computer could accept a new procedure in the midst of a computation and adjust its calculations accordingly. The machine would then follow the modified procedure, and even alter the algorithm itself when required. In other words, the automaton could be programmed at will, a capability which would lead the way to the development of the general purpose computer.

The next major step for informatics took the form of integrated circuits. The use of semiconductors to process data on a small chip led to the demise of the vacuum tube, and the emergence of slimmer, swifter devices. The trend toward smaller, lighter, and faster platforms continues to this day.

In the realm of communications, a watershed arose from the networking experiments of the 1960s. At the height of the Cold War, the U.S. sought to develop a robust network to ensure the survival of communication facilities in the event of a nuclear strike by the Soviet Union. The result was a flexible system of linking computers which came to be known as the Internet architecture.

A Net is Born. In 1962, the U.S. Air Force commissioned a study to develop a new type of communication network. The hallmark of the system would be the ability to withstand a nuclear attack. Even if any site or city in America were destroyed, the network would function well enough to launch a counterstrike.

The study was conducted by a government think tank known as RAND. The upshot of the investigation was a recommendation for a failsafe scheme based on decentralized control. This could be achieved by splitting a message into small chunks and routing them on the fly. At each node in the network, the routing decision would be made by an autonomous computer which would favor one link over any other based on current conditions in its neighborhood.

In 1968, the Advanced Research Projects Agency (ARPA) within the U.S. Department of Defense awarded a contract to build a pilot network using the decentralized scheme. The infrastructure, called ARPANET, was constructed the following year. The prototype network linked four sites: three institutes of research and education in California plus one in Utah.

The network served as a platform for novel services. The first program for electronic mail was created in 1972. This was the work of Ray Tomlinson at Bolt Beranek and Newman, a technology development firm in Massachusetts.

The following year, plans were made for a robust set of communication standards. These conventions were later to be called the Transmission Control Protocol (TCP) and the Internet Protocol (IP). The project was spearheaded by Vinton G. Cerf at Stanford University and Robert E. Kahn at DARPA (the same agency as ARPA, but renamed with a prefix "D" for "Defense"). In 1974, the term *Internet* was coined in a paper presenting the Transmission Control Protocol.

The Internet continued to evolve over the ensuing years. Additional utilities came online, such as tools for searching files in large repositories. Despite the advances, however, the network remained an arcane resource for technologists and researchers at assorted sites around the world.

A breakout occurred in 1989, when the British software engineer Tim Berners-Lee proposed a hypertext system called the World Wide Web. The collection of standards would allow users around the globe to pool their knowledge in a matrix of linked documents. The next year, a prototype browser for the Web was written and tested at the European Center for Nuclear Research in Geneva.

In 1991, the program was released to the Internet community at large. This event marked the dawn of the second generation of the Net, when access to online resources would become a routine feature of everyday life.

A centralized system cannot function properly if the dominant computer is inoperative. On the other hand, a decentralized platform with multiple connections among the nodes may continue to function merrily even after several machines in the network have collapsed. The distributed scheme relies on the coordination of activities among peer-level machines.

In addition to high reliability, the decentralized architecture of the Internet can embrace additional computers without the need to modify the basic structure or behavior of existing machines. Over the years, the organic structure of the network has comfortably accommodated the explosive growth of the information highway.

Open standards. Until the 1980s, most computers were islands of information processing. Designed as stand-alone devices, computers at the time had little or no ability to communicate with other machines.

Moreover, computer systems were incompatible in terms of both hardware and software. In general the incoherence of systems applied not only between manufacturers, but also for products from a single vendor. For instance, a program written for one line of hardware would not run properly — or sometimes at all — on another product family from the same vendor.

The incompatibility of product lines in parallel with galloping advances in technology led to maddening complexity. Sophisticated information systems would take years to implement, even as they routinely exceeded their budgeted funds and planning horizons. To add insult and mayhem to fiscal injury, the resulting systems usually failed to fulfill their sponsors' objectives.

By the beginning of the 80s, the revolt of computer users against quirky products reached epidemic proportions. In response to the uprising, vendors of hardware and software began to take steps toward compatibility. After decades of hesitation, the vendors made headway in developing user-friendly products and establishing industry forums to promote universal formats. The trickle of open standards turned into a river in the early 90s as a result of external developments: the rise of the World Wide Web plus the adoption of email for commercial messaging.

Since then, the river has cascaded into a torrent with the full commercialization of the Internet. Open standards and the Web in particular became the norm for information access by all types of users.

At the same time, organizations began to shift their operations into cyberspace in order to coordinate transactions between enterprises as well as automate activities within a single firm.

New enterprises emerged on the digital landscape and captured the hearts of both Netizens and financial markets. Some ventures were upstarts. As a case in point, the online bookseller Amazon.com popped out of nowhere and took on mature companies in a staid industry.

Other ventures were sheer novelty, given life by the digital medium. A landmark of the virtual firmament was found in Yahoo, a portal for visitors to cyberspace.

The expansion of encryption schemes and security measures on the Net laid the groundwork for mass commercialization. By the turn of the century, shopping in cyberia was to be a routine experience for increasing numbers of consumers.

Meanwhile, virtuality became a standard goal for organizations around the planet. The Internet turned into a digital grail as one enterprise after another rallied to the flag of cyberization.

The Net was seen as a highway to growth and agility for both individual firms and entire economies. Digitopia was more than just a promised land: all who failed to cross into the world of the ethereal would wither in the shriveling wastes of the old.

Nowhere was the faith stronger than in the capital markets. Here investors came to value virtual ventures — even those losing money by the barrel — solely on faith. In the new religion, an Internet company could be worth thousands more than a "brick-and-mortar" enterprise, even if the number of employees were only a tiny fraction of a mature rival's, and with little or no revenues to match its infant status.

Despite the spell of euphoria, investors regained their senses in the spring of 2000. Online ventures floating on hype came crashing earthward, and many disintegrated in the aftermath.

On the other hand, a few of the digital startups were surely destined to justify their generous valuations in the long run. But which ones? The winners would stand out in sharp relief only with the passage of time.

Meanwhile, the pilgrimage continues. Clearly every member of a knowledge based society has to trek to cyberland as a part-time visitor if not a full-time resident. This is as true for the individual as for the organization.

The only real question is when and how to commune with unreal space. For this purpose, the small book in your hands has been designed as a guide to exploration: to chart the terrain, view the transports, and plant some pointers for the trek ahead.

Compass of the Book

This introductory chapter has presented the background and arraigned the key issues to be probed throughout the book. The second chapter will examine in greater detail the basic technologies of the Internet as well as the foundations of multimedia and smart software.

The maturation of machine learning over the past decade has paved the way for digital agents which can serve as aides in cyberspace. In response to a query from a user, a smart agent can roam the Net, retrieve the nuggets, and filter the results. Moreover, the software can tailor a presentation to the needs of the moment as well as the user's evolving level of expertise. The skills of customization may be realized through procedures such as neural networks, case based reasoning, and inductive logic. These adaptive technologies are discussed in Chapter 2.

The third chapter examines the practical impact of the digital techniques. Ideas once tenuous have sprouted into a lush field of goods and services flowering in the digital economy.

The fourth chapter examines the consequences of the technologies for commerce and industry. The full spectrum of managerial functions must be reconsidered for electronic business, ranging from product conception and marketing research to global distribution and customer service.

The ferment in digitopia underscores the need for a systematic approach to scoping markets and crafting strategies. The creation of a competitive strategy is the target of Chapter 5.

The penultimate chapter explores a variety of tools and applications which will play a prominent role in the second wave of the digital quake. Over the next decade or so, these technologies will find their way into everyday life at home, school, and office.

The final chapter peers far into the future to explore a number of themes on the drawing boards and off the map. One development lies in autonomous systems which can learn and evolve without human intervention. Complex systems often exhibit emergent properties which take even their creators by surprise. One day, adaptive systems will reach beyond the limits set by their own programmers.

Another capability which will come to the fore stems from the extension of the Net beyond Mother Earth. The interplanetary version of the Internet will take flight with the new generation of spacecraft slated for Mars.

The appendices provide a handful of materials to complement the body of the text. In particular, the first attachment offers a tutorial on the basics of digital media and Internet standards. The survey may be used as an orientation before reading Chapter 2, or a reference afterwards.

Today, informatic technologies are indispensable tools for success, whether in the hands of the individual on the job or the enterprise in the marketplace. Unfortunately, a hefty fraction — perhaps an overwhelming majority—of large-scale projects have disappointed their corporate champions in the past. As it happens, the enormous scope and restless nature of digital techniques tend to render targets elusive, thereby proving projects to be as intractable in the millennium as in the previous century.

On the other hand, the sporadic examples of successful deployment reveal that the sophistication of a novel technology is not always a crippling burden. Rather, more failures are known to result from organizational hurdles than from technical constraints. Experience over the past few decades points toward a set of design rules for comprehensive projects. A distillation of winsome policies for crafting an informatic strategy is the focus of Appendix B.

In centuries past, a person's life and career were fixed almost entirely by his or her father's station in life. The daughter of a king would become a princess, while the son of a serf would remain a vassal. A subject could not change his vocation at will; for a peasant to become a king was the stuff of fairy tales.

By the beginning of the 20th century, however, destiny had become choice. A farmer's daughter could not plausibly aspire to be princess, but she could become a teacher, doctor, mortician, or even a politician if that were her inclination.

While the selection of a profession was a matter of choice, the subsequent career path remained largely a straightjacket. By the 1970s, professionals in the United States might change jobs and addresses every few years, but they tended to remain within a single discipline.

All this began to change, however, in the ensuing decades. Rapid advances in every field led to the swift obsolescence of knowledge, which in turn eroded the relative advantage of old timers in professions everywhere.

The job market became more fluid, and individuals began to pursue multiple careers over the course of a single lifetime. Even within a particular discipline, it became imperative to keep up with new developments which would pop up at an accelerating rate.

As a result, continuing education blossomed and entered the mainstream. Today, individuals and organizations invest billions of dollars annually in part-time coursework, on-the-job training, professional conferences, and executive seminars. Lifelong education is no longer a luxury for the idiosyncratic few, but a necessity for all productive citizens.

Each actor in a digital economy has to update his skills continually through formal channels such as coursework as well as informal means including ad hoc study. The potential for networks, multimedia, and smart agents to support educational objectives is immense. Unfortunately, most projects in online education have thus far failed to take full advantage of the varied technologies. Rather, the majority of programs in virtual instruction have relied largely on communication through email, chat rooms, and static documents rather than real-time interaction through multisensory modes.

The state of vanguard programs for virtual pedagogy is the subject of Appendix C. The attachment explores the ways in which digital methods can enhance the educational process and bolster personal skills in a society of knowledge.

Adept programs can support not only pedagogical goals, but the entire gamut of human endeavors. Appendix D delves further into the field of knowledge discovery than is presented in Chapter 2. The supplement explores tools for data mining at various levels of knowledge acquisition as well as their deployment in personal interfaces for surfers of all stripes, skills, and slants.

Next in line, Appendix E provides a diverse collection of exercises to flesh out the concepts in the body of the text. The problems range from basic practice in the use of the Web to hands-on lessons for wielding software tools. Moreover, the design projects in the attachment offer frameworks for integrating and digesting the assortment of ideas in the book.

The final appendix presents a cornucopia of resources on the Web. The spread of treats includes links to news services as well as introductory surveys which complement the discussion in this book. Moreover, an array of specialized sites offers weighty tools with which to dig into assorted topics in greater detail.

But first things first. According to the default agenda in the book's outline, the next chapter presents an overview of the enabling technologies for our collective journey into cyberspace.

Lady or gentleman, please fasten your seat belt . . . and thank you for choosing to read with us.

Chapter 2

Technologies in Cyberia

Day by day our digital society becomes more dynamic, abstruse, and global. For the most part, our grandparents lived in rustic settings with a leisurely pace to match. In those days, the scope of concern rarely stretched beyond the neighborhood and the municipality. The central government was a distant authority which proscribed the outer boundaries of human interaction through a sparse set of laws. Foreign cultures were an enigma and adjacent countries lay a world apart.

The abstractions of yesteryear, however, have materialized by degrees into the palpables today. Through satellite channels we monitor remote crises as they unfold; via digital links we debate burning issues in online meetings; through regional trade we savor vittles harvested by foreign hands; in worldwide markets we repulse pirates half a globe apart.

The 20th century has wrought sweeping changes in the activities of the organization as well as the individual. Yesterday an enterprise could focus on its domestic market and conduct business with the speed of airmailed letters. Today, the same firm is likely to interact online with business partners, converse in real-time with customers, and compete constantly against offshore rivals.

The need for connectivity and responsiveness has powered the explosive growth of the Internet since the 1990s. On the technical side, the reasons for the popularity of the Internet lie in the open architecture, decentralized control, and interoperability among diverse platforms of hardware and software. The ascent of the global infobahn has accelerated even further with the advent of the World Wide Web.

The expansion of electronic links, the emergence of data warehouses, and the imperative of ever-swifter response underscore the utility of intelligent tools to assist in decision making.[2] The need for capable aid applies throughout the day, ranging from work and study to play and travel.

In the larger context, our society is grinding through a structural change as a result of leaps in technology and the expansion of global commerce. These effects are interlinked: technologies such as the Internet facilitate international trade, while the globalization of resources spurs technical progress.

This book focuses on digital technologies and their uses. Yet the interplay of technology and society cannot be entirely ignored. For this reason, the discussion in the trunk of the book as well as the appendices takes account of the global reach and impact of informatic systems.

As the digital revolution gathers force, the planet will gradually metamorphose into a single virtual Web. Electronic scouts and autonomous probes have begun to explore the bottom of the sea and the expanse of outer space. By the middle of the 21st century, the Internet will stretch from the depths of terra firma to the ends of the solar system.

Information Highway

Back in the early 1990s, it was the fashion for self-proclaimed visionaries to predict the imminent arrival of an information highway which would transform life and society. By the middle of the decade, however, these swamis gradually came to realize that the infobahn had already arrived. In fact, researchers around the world had been quietly using the Internet for decades to collaborate with colleagues on the far side of the planet and to schedule lunch appointments with friends across the campus.

The Internet is a network of basic networks which communicate through a common set of standards. The exponential growth of the Internet can be attributed to a variety of factors:

- Open standards and the ease of connecting to the extant network
- Tradition of liberal information exchange
- Little or no direct cost to individual users
- High reliability

The strength of the Internet springs from the dispersion of control. The decentralized scheme relies on a clutch of versatile conventions. In particular, the basic mechanism for coordinating the system is a standard known as the Internet Protocol, or IP.

To send an electronic document across the network, the file is first split into a string of small pieces, each of which is called a *data packet*. Every packet is then capped with a *header* which includes a variety of information such as its order in the sequence of dispatches and its ultimate destination.

The transmission of a message along the network is supervised through a related standard known as the Transport Control Protocol, or TCP. At the final destination, the packets are assembled into the proper sequence based on information in their header segments.

The networking procedures ensure that each packet follows an efficient route from the source computer to the final target. To illustrate, suppose that a message is to be sent from San Francisco to New York. One way to route it might be from San Francisco to Chicago, then on to New York. However, suppose that the communication line to the Midwest is laboring under heavy traffic at the moment, or that the computer at Chicago is temporarily out of service. Then the network protocol could decide on the fly to route the packet first to Austin, Texas. Subsequently, the computer at Austin might send it directly on to New York, or first to Miami or some other waystation, depending on the status of the overall network at the time. In this way, the protocol ensures the efficient use of the network in spite of fluctuating circumstances.

By employing an open set of conventions, the Internet standards accommodate all types of equipment, whether in the form of hardware or software. The universal interfaces ensure the compatibility of machines ranging from mainframes to smartphones, and supervisory software from Windows to Unix and the Macintosh.

In the parlance of cyberia, a *host* is a computer connected to the Internet. In order to route messages properly, each host is assigned a unique number known as the Internet Protocol Number, or IPN. This is analogous to each person on Earth having a unique telephone address. A conventional phone number comprises several components: country code, area code, exchange, and local index. An example might be the number 1-212-749-1000 for someone living in New York.

In an analogous way, an Internet Protocol Number has four components, as exemplified by the following sequence: 123.456.765.432. The first two numbers (that is, 123 and 456) identify the network, while the last two specify the host computer within that network.

Since a list of numbers is difficult for humans to remember, it is possible to use an alias known as a *domain name*. For instance, when a user types the address

yahoo.com

into his Web browser, the alphabetic name will be converted automatically to its corresponding IP Number. This conversion is performed by a computer known as a Domain Name Server (DNS).

To reach a house within a walled city in medieval times, a traveler first had to pass through the outer gates. In a similar way, to reach a host computer on a particular network, a message must first pass through an electronic portal. In the digital lingo, the guardian of the entrance is a computer called a *gateway*.

The transmission of a data packet across a network requires the services of a *router*. The latter machine is a computer which directs a package to an adjacent gateway, depending on the location of the final host and the condition of the network in the immediate locale at the time.

The Internet serves as the foundation for a rich variety of services ranging from electronic mail to online chat. A number of the most popular utilities are as follows.

The Simple Mail Transfer Protocol (SMTP) is a basic vehicle for conveying electronic mail. The beauty of SMTP lies in simplicity due to its ease of implementation and use. But we know that beauty is only skin deep. Being lightweight, the protocol is not equipped for fancier tasks such as attaching an external file to an email note. A protocol with greater substance is found in the Multipart Internet Mail Encoding (MIME) standard, which is the convention used by modern browsers.

On the other hand, MIME lacks discretion, as it does not allow for the encryption of messages. This limitation has been overcome by a secure version of the MIME protocol, known simply as SMIME. The use of SMIME has become more prevalent as commerce on the Internet expands, in line with increasing transfers of financial and personal data across public networks.

World Wide Web

In addition to electronic mail, the vehicle which brought the Internet into the mainstream of society lies in the World Wide Web (WWW). The Web is a virtual lattice of documents residing on Internet hosts. This global network is based on three primary standards.

- HyperText Transfer Protocol (HTTP), a convention for exchanging documents.
- Uniform Resource Locator (URL), a standard to pinpoint the location of a document anywhere on the global network.
- HyperText Markup Language (HTML), a convention for formatting multimedia documents and providing virtual links to other files.

An alluring aspect of the Web lies in the ability to handle *hypertext*: a document which contains online links to other sections in the same file or to external files. Another plus is found in the ability to present media in multiple formats.

The Web provides ready access to documents scattered all over the globe. A machine which requests a document or a service from an online resource is called a *client*; the computer which fulfills the request is known as a *server*. On the Net, the HyperText Transfer Protocol is the convention used for transmissions between a program residing on a client and the server on the Web which responds to the request. An example of client software is found in the Navigator browser from Netscape Communications.

The standard for formatting a document on a Web browser is the HyperText Markup Language. The language specifies a set of labels to describe the layout, appearance, or function of an object on a page.

A *tag* is a higher-level prescription which assigns a property or behavior to an item on a page. For instance, a pair of tags might specify that the enclosed text is to be presented in bold.

Consider the following line in an HTML document:

Help me! I'm <i> trapped </i> behind <b> this page!! </b>

The tags <i> and </i> indicate that the flanked text should be italicized, while the duo of <b> and </b> calls for bold font. A Web browser which encounters this line would interpret the text as follows.

Help me! I'm *trapped* behind **this page**!!

Other features of HTML include tags to generate tables with ease, or to specify a particular color for the background in a window.

A hallmark of a Web document is the *anchor* which links an item on a page to an external object. For instance, clicking on an image might lead to the presentation of a tune, while selecting a different item could lead to a movie.

The location of each document on the Net is specified by a convention known as the Uniform Resource Locator. To illustrate, consider the following URL:

www.mit.edu/report.html

The address specifies a file named *report.html* which resides on the main host at the Massachusetts Institute of Technology. Upon receiving the spec from any machine on the Net, the server will transmit a copy of the report to the client if conditions permit. Of course, the server may be unable or unwilling to comply with the request. Such a document might not exist, or is a confidential file accessible only from an intramural browser, and so on.

In addition to ordinary documents, a Web server can provide ready access to other information sources such as a database management system. For this purpose, a server can interact with an application program via a standard known as the Common Gateway Interface (CGI). When a client submits a query, the target server can use the interface to process the request.

CGI is a relatively simple protocol for running programs on a Web server. The convention is often employed in parallel with independent programs written in a general-purpose language such as Java. The latter is a full-fledged language designed for use on networks of heterogeneous computers. A program written in Java can act as a stand-alone application.

Java can also be used in a supporting role for another program. A simple example is found in a module to check for typos in a digital form employed by an order processing package. A small Java program in an auxiliary role is known as an *applet.*

When deployed as a supportive applet on the Web, a procedure in Java is first converted into a compact format known as *byte code.* The code is then transferred from the server to a Web browser. Finally, the applet is executed by the browser software while simulating a virtual computer which understands Java code.

A multimedia system can incorporate additional capabilities such as artificial intelligence, online databases, and mobile networking. The need for deft interfaces springs from the fact that content is scrambling into massive databases at a frenzied rate. In addition to the sheer volume of material, the knowledge in a data warehouse can take diverse forms ranging from text and pictures to audio and video.

Media as You Like It

The advantage of multimedia lies in its affinity with human cognition. Since a picture can replace a myriad words, multimedia allows for swift comprehension. The use of sight, sound, and motion captures the user's attention and provides an assortment of cues for subsequent recall.

Digital media can also support interactivity: as an active participant rather than a passive viewer, the user becomes more involved with the content. Moreover, real-time interaction opens the door to tailoring a presentation to the changing tastes of each user.

Traditional types of multimedia range from text and graphics to animation and video. An interactive mode takes the form of *virtual reality*: a realistic environment simulated by a computer. The technology appeals simultaneously to a variety of sensory channels, ranging from three-dimensional vistas to stereophonic sound.

In the olden days, synthetic worlds were deployed only on isolated systems such as stand-alone workstations. Since the mid-1990s, 3-dimensional objects could be rendered on the Net using the Virtual Reality Modeling Language (VRML). The language can be employed, for instance, to create an artificial world in which a prospective customer can "test drive" a car and evaluate its performance prior to purchase.

On certain game consoles, a joystick with force feedback can simulate tactile sensations. Other mechanisms to accommodate the sense of touch include data gloves with mechanical actuators which initiate or resist the movement of the fingers.

Virtual reality is not restricted to the visual, auditory, and tactile senses. Commercial products to address olfaction appeared in the 1990s. The general approach involves the storage of a score of chemical vials at the user's site. The fragrance in each vial is then released through control signals synchronized with a multimedia presentation, such as a movie shown on digital television.

Without doubt, some ingenious entrepreneur will cook up analogous schemes to appeal to the taste buds. Before long, a visitor to cyberspace is likely to find himself enclosed in a body suit with apparatus to manipulate all the senses.

A software *agent* is a procedure which acts on behalf of a human or another program. Depending on its functionality, an agent may operate autonomously or under a tight leash.

A virtual representative of a user is known as an *avatar*. One of the most popular destinations for avatars is located in a community known as the Contact Consortium. Here Netizens can interact with each other in a variety of online worlds ranging from indoor cafes to outdoor parks.

The invasion of realspace by aliens from bitspace began before the turn of the century. The first landing stage lay in the field of entertainment via roles ranging from chatting and modeling to singing and dancing.

An example of a synthetic personality is found in Webbie Tookay ("Web 2K"), a fashion model who exists only in cyberspace. The model, whose physique is an idealized but realistic rendition of a 17-year old, was born of a joint venture between Elite Models and Illusion 2K of Brazil. The virtual Venus was designed for appearances on TV ads, Websites, online games, and other electric venues.

A pet in the real world is partly autonomous and partially reliant on its owner. In the digital realm, the PostPet is a virtual character for delivering email. Developed by Sony Communication Network in 1997, the program incorporates adaptive capabilities through artificial intelligence. A digital pet takes the form of a critter such as a cat, dog, or tortoise. The pet learns to write email to its owner, or to other pets and their owners. Moreover, pets can befriend fellow creatures in a virtual park and thereby pave the way for their respective owners to get acquainted. In this way, the software serves as a medium for making real friends through unreal space.

A user can choose to pat or hit his own pet, or other messengers that have come to deliver mail. If an owner mistreats his pet too often, it will run away – never to return. As it happens, even a spoiled pet will die after 2 or 3 years. Since it cannot be resurrected, Sony is forced to sell another copy of the program to any bereaved owner who desires a replacement.

Over 100,000 copies of PostPet were sold between November 1997 and April 1998 alone. By early 2000, PostPet had an online fan club of hundreds of thousands of users in Japan.

As illustrated by the popularity of the PostPet, fellowship is a prime attraction of cyberville. A gaggle of chatting services have sprung up on the Net to cater to this market.

For individual users, the applications of online interaction range from socializing and entertainment to project coordination and foreign language practice. Organizational applications of the technology span the gamut from conference calls and distance learning to online collaboration and customer service.

By the eve of the millennium, smart agents began to serve as aides to support customer interactions. An example of a program for customer service is found at Lucas Arts, a game vendor in San Rafael, California. The software, named Yoda, interacts with users through a natural language interface. The agent handles about 1,000 queries each day, thereby bearing the workload of 33 human representatives in the customer service department.

Channels to Freedom

Until recently, the standard doorway to cyberspace took the form of a personal computer. Today, increasing numbers of users are crossing the threshold with portable gadgets ranging from digital organizers to smart watches.

The global standard for accessing the mobile Net is found in the Wireless Application Protocol, also known as the Wireless *Access* Protocol (WAP). According to the WAP Forum, an industry consortium, the use of handsets for Net access was slated to outstrip that of PC's within the first few years of the millennium.

Since portable devices such as smartphones have petite display screens, they cannot comfortably handle ordinary Web pages of the sort which appear on desktop computers. To accommodate the smaller display area, a mobile device can instead use a convention known as the Wireless Markup Language (WML). The language is designed for displays on a pint-sized screen, as well as input through keystrokes using a single handful of fingers.

The Wireless Markup Language is one convention for formatting content for display on a mobile device. Its role is analogous to that of the HyperText Markup Language for presenting a Web page on a full-sized screen.

A second convention for presenting material on diminutive screens is found in the standard known as Compact HTML, or CHTML. This language is mostly a subset of the regular HTML format, but with expanded features for specifying audio interactions, whether in the form of speech or music.

The content on a conventional Web display can be animated through a simple programming language known as JavaScript. The analogue for programming a mobile device is found in a compact standard: the Wireless Markup Language Script, better known by the awkward name of WMLScript. Although similar in syntax and function to JavaScript, the wireless version is less demanding on the skimpy processor and memory units on a mobile device.

The use of unwired gadgets has expanded even faster than the growth of the Internet. According to industry estimates, several hundred million wireless devices populated the planet by the end of 2000. Within several years, billions of mobile subscribers were expected to roam the globe.

The first excursions into wireless commerce were largely the province of pioneers in Scandinavia. A case in point is Handelsbanken, the largest bank in the Nordic region. This enterprise was the first bank to demonstrate a financial application of the Wireless Application Protocol. In October 1999, the company initiated tests with selected customers, providing them with smartphones from Nokia and Ericsson. From the outset, a user could obtain stock market data and inquire about his personal portfolio. Shortly thereafter, a customer could use his cellphone to review accounts, transfer money, and buy stocks.

Gleaning Knowledge from Data

The past few decades have witnessed increasing interest in tools to generate new knowledge. The realm of *knowledge discovery* is an outgrowth of the fields of machine learning, statistics, and visualization schemes.

The 1980s saw great strides in adaptive methods including neural networks, genetic algorithms, and inductive reasoning. However, it was only in the final decade of the century that the cost and speed of personal computers had progressed sufficiently to support the widespread adoption of data mining tools.

During the 1990s, leading organizations around the planet launched initiatives to implement data warehouses. A data warehouse serves as an integrated repository of records by unifying digital systems for design, marketing, accounting, and other functions.

A data warehouse is an arsenal of information. By itself, however, a warehouse can do little more than support conventional operations in accounting, scheduling, and so on. These functions correspond to the same type of business applications and software techniques first developed in the 1960s.

The real promise of a data warehouse lies in its potential as the raw material for fresh knowledge. The quest for new knowledge is the sphere of data mining, which can support diverse activities ranging from business planning and portfolio management to engineering design and product development.

Knowledge mining tools are used to discover useful patterns, trends or relations in databases.[3] The automated approach to knowledge discovery is especially helpful when dealing with sprawling data sets or complex relationships. For many applications, automated software may find subtle patterns which escape the notice of manual analysis, or whose complexity exceeds the cognitive abilities of humans. Secondly, software for data mining may ensure the practicality of analyzing large datasets which would require an unjustifiable amount of manual effort. Thirdly, automated procedures may monitor complex environments such as online markets on a continuous basis, updating their knowledge base immediately with the outbreak of new developments.

The appeal of learning schemes lies in their superiority over traditional techniques. In particular, knowledge based methods tend to outperform statistical models in tasks ranging from classification to forecasting.

The field of knowledge mining is still in its youth, but has already yielded a bounteous crop. For example, learning programs have rummaged through corporate databases to identify distinct clusters of customers, thereby allowing firms to develop targeted marketing programs. In the financial sector, knowledge discovery has been used by loan departments to identify the profiles of probable defaulters. The future looks even brighter for data mining as it comes to play a leading role in other fields such as scientific research, medical diagnosis, and crime prevention.

Statistics. Statistical schemes represent a long-standing approach to acquiring insight into the nature of a data set.[4] On the other hand, *statistical methods* such as regression, factor analysis, and other techniques tend to focus on simple structures known as linear models.

As a result, their applicability to the complex relations of the real world remains limited. For instance, statistical procedures by themselves are unequal to the task of forecasting a stock market index. In data mining applications, the tools of statistics are used to complement autolearning techniques. An example lies in statistical methods for automatically grouping records in a database into clusters of similar cases. This capability is employed, for instance, in classifying customers into different levels of profitability and thus priority for the marketing department.

Neural network. Perhaps the most popular scheme for data mining is found in the neural model. A *neural network* is a program motivated by the information processing activities of the human brain. The key attraction of the neural model lies in the autonomous discovery of salient relationships in a database.

Another strength is found in robustness, also known by the term *graceful degradation*. To illustrate the notion of sturdiness, consider a neural network which has been trained properly, but fed incorrect data for a new problem. If the input data is only slightly askew, then the output from the neural net is likely to go awry in only a minor way. This property stands in stark contrast to a number of other software techniques such as expert systems, in which small errors in input can easily produce large errors in output.

The most common type of neural network uses a learning procedure known as *backpropagation*. Once trained properly, a backpropagation model produces a reliable response to any problem within its scope of expertise.[5]

Despite their strengths, neural nets suffer from a number of limitations such as the lengthy period required to learn a task. Another drawback lies in the implicit nature of the acquired knowledge, which cannot be easily fathomed by a human decision maker.

This last limitation is analogous to that of the human brain. For instance, I happen to know that London is the capital of the United Kingdom. On the other hand, a surgeon who were to open up my head would be unable to find that knowledge emblazoned anywhere amongst the gray matter.

In a comparable way, a neural net might produce accurate results without revealing the underlying logic. For this reason, a human user could feel uneasy about the outcome.

In practice, a neural net is often deployed as a source for suggestions rather than as a final arbiter. This role is exemplified by a financial aide which offers suggestions to a human principal rather than trading stocks on its own. As the technology of data mining improves, however, autonomous programs are assuming more decisive roles in every field of endeavor.

Case based reasoning. A learning system should make increasingly useful decisions as it accumulates experience. To this end, one of the most versatile approaches to adaptation lies in *case based reasoning* (CBR). The methodology enables a software agent to learn from experience and enhance its knowledge base during the course of its duties.

To illustrate, CBR can be used to support the task of design by reminding an engineer of previous examples which bear on a new problem. This is actually the norm in product design by a human. In the realm of technology, for instanse, an engineer learns basic skills in school and acquires proficiency through years of practice.

For most of the 20th century, engineering projects often relied on quantitative models of the problem domain, whether analyzing the breaking point of a bridge or portraying the airflow around a fuselage. Although mathematical methods for scrutinizing a design can be useful for programming computers, they are not necessarily effective as models of human thinking in crafting a prototype.

Case based reasoning provides a linkage between the precise models in a computer program and the informal practice of designers who rely on prior design situations. The approach in CBR may be viewed as a form of analogy, where previous problems or experiences provide insight toward potential solutions. In particular, an engineer might be reminded of a prior solution to cooling a computer chip when designing a new generation of computers. The decision maker uses analogy to resolve a new problem by associating it with an earlier case.

The recall of a design first involves the search for a relevant case from the database of similar problems and solutions. Next, the adaptive phase of design involves the recognition of differences between the selected instance and the target problem, followed by the modification of the earlier solution to resolve the new problem.

Case based reasoning has been deployed in a broad spectrum of domains. The applications range from everyday tasks such as story telling and meal planning to commercial fields such as product design and market forecasting.

A key advantage of case based reasoning lies in the ability to work with data in their original format. The CBR methodology can be effective even if the knowledge base is imperfect; for instance, when a database is incomplete or contaminated with noise.

One drawback, however, lies in the tendency of CBR tools to identify similarities based on superficial rather than substantive features of two cases. For instance, a program might decide that economic growth for Euroland next year will be similar to that in North America, simply because the populations and precipitation for the two regions are comparable this year. On the other hand, the risk of faulty reasoning is a perennial hazard applicable to any learning system, whether digital or human.

Genetic algorithm. A *genetic algorithm*, also known by its initials GA, is a procedure modeled after the processes of biological evolution and population dynamics. In essence, the procedure selects highly fit individuals, then mixes their chromosomes at random to yield variegated offspring. Within the subsequent population, the unfit are eliminated while the hardy are culled as sources of genetic material for the next generation.

Traditional methods of optimization tend to pursue a single path toward the goal by determining the best direction at each step. In contrast, a GA throws up several potential solutions in parallel, then modifies them in a random fashion to yield the subsequent step toward the target. The inherent parallelism and the advantage of random search, thoughtfully guided, permits the use of genetic algorithms for tackling many formidable problems.[6]

As part of the genetic procedure, the individuals in a population are evaluated through a measure of superiority which indicates their relative worth. The fittest individuals are then chosen for further processing.

The concept of biological inheritance is implemented by selecting two fit individuals and *crossing* or mixing their chromosomes. The crossover operation involves two steps: slicing each chromosome at a random location, then recombining corresponding sections from the original strands.

Another way to effect variation in the population takes the form of whimsical aberration. In the process of *mutation,* a location on a chromosome is selected arbitrarily and its symbol changed at random to another feasible value.

A particular sequence of symbols for a chromosome is called a *genotype.* At times two different genotypes may exhibit the same appearance or behavior; in that case they constitute a single *phenotype.* For instance, a critter might inherit two genes for brown fur from its parents, thereby growing brown hair as it matures. On the other hand, its cousin may inherit a gene for black hair and another for blond, and subsequently end up with brown hair as well. The two offspring have different genotypes but the same phenotype in the context of hair color.

On occasion, a population may reach a dead end in evolutionary terms. With insufficient variety in the common pool of genes, the evolutionary process becomes "congested" and the population cannot progress further.

To illustrate, a small pair of cuspid teeth may be adequate for survival on a vegetarian diet, and optimal for the feeding habits of their owner. On the other hand, a couple of huge canines would help an animal in an auxiliary vocation as a carnivore and thereby diversify its diet. Meanwhile, a middling size of spikes could be neither here nor there: too small to pitch into fleeing prey and merely a nuisance for nibbling on veggies. The "dead zone" of mediocrity between small and large dentation presents a barrier to progressive adaptation. A creature which acquires genes for intermediate canines may well perish before it passes on its trait to the subsequent generation, thereby aborting the trend toward a gradual increase in size. For this adaptation, only an abrupt leap from the local optimum of dainty cuspids to that of wolfish canines will deliver the species to the Eldorado of fearsome fangs and tartare cuisine.

A mutation can effect a metamorphosis at a single stroke, thereby allowing a population to escape a cozy but inferior optimum and vault instead into pristine realms in search of a global optimum. The rate of mutation must be high enough to avoid long periods of stagnation in the evolutionary process, but low enough to ensure a measure of stability; that is, providing the population with a chance to reach the local optimum before leaping into distant terrain.

The appropriate type and extent of mutation as well as crossover, will of course depend on the domain. In practical applications of genetic algorithms, the characteristics of the problem domain are usually too complex to pin down in advance. For this reason, the optimal configuration of the fitness function as well as the nature of crossover and mutation are design issues which must be guided by a knowledge of the application area plus experience with adaptive schemes.

Genetic algorithms have been deployed in diverse settings. These range from work scheduling and product design to process control and financial forecasting.

A genetic procedure offers a resilient approach to problem solving. On the other hand, a GA can be excruciatingly slow as it plods through myriads of potential solutions in parallel. A genetic algorithm is a great slug, surpassing even a neural network in torpor.

The lethargy has dampened enthusiasm for deploying genetic methods in many practical domains. On the other hand, the relentless advance of computing power will continue to lower the barriers for genetic procedures.

Inductive learning. *Induction* refers to the generation of criteria to classify objects based on a collection of examples. The procedure generates new knowledge in the form of decision rules or branching trees.[7]

In the inductive approach, a set of training examples serves as input to the learning program. During the training phase, the description of a group, also called a *class*, is inferred from the available records. Each example takes the form of a case which is represented by a list of attributes.

The cases can be organized into a hierarchy – also known as a *tree* – using concepts from the field of information theory. Every node within the tree represents a decision point. Each branch below a node then indicates an option or pathway.

The knowledge organized in an inductive tree can be used to determine, for instance, whether a manufactured device with a particular set of features is normal or defective. In a similar way, current conditions in a financial market can be analyzed to discern which stocks will rise and others fall over the course of the month.

Induction is a versatile technique in which solutions are obtained through a process of search and generalization. However, the methodology can be cumbersome to use and has not been deployed as widely as it deserves.

Multiple schemes. Until the turn of the century, applications of knowledge mining tended to employ single techniques in isolation. However, each scheme has its advantages and drawbacks. For this reason, a multistrategy approach to knowledge mining provides a way to harness the strengths of various techniques while bypassing the limitations of each method.

There are many ways to integrate elementary schemes. For example, one might use the output from a case based reasoning module in conjunction with a neural network.

A limitation of the multistrategy approach lies in the fact that the technology is still in its youth. Even so, the field will mature rapidly in the years ahead. The effectiveness of compound methods has been demonstrated in realms ranging from the prediction of genomic function to the augury of economic growth.[8] In time, hybrid techniques for knowledge mining will permeate the entire gamut of human activity, thereby enhancing productivity at the level of the individual user as well as the overall economy.

Wrapup. An overview of learning tools and tasks may be presented in terms of a 2-dimensional framework. Table 2.1 presents a chart with axes relating to function and technique. The functional dimension covers the categories of prediction, classification, rule generation, decision trees, dependency relations, statistical summarization, and visualization. On the other hand, the dimension of technique comprises the neural network, case based reasoning, induction, genetic algorithm, statistics, and compound schemes.

Table 2.1. Typology of data mining tools by function and technique. Each item in a cell denotes an example of a pertinent tool.9

METHOD FUNCTION	Neural network	CBR	Induction	Genetic algorithm	Statistics	Compound scheme
Prediction	• Neural Connection • Recon	• KATE	• KATE	• Generator • Ultragem	• Qualitec-4 (Orthogonal arrays)	• Second order learning
Classification	• MATLAB Neural Toolbox • Inspect • Neural Connection	• ECOBWEB • KATE	• SE-learn • OC1 • MLC++ • DBlearn	• Ultragem • Evolver	• SPSS • CHAID • Auto Class C	• Inspect • Darwin • Clementine • Modelware • Weka
Rule generation	• Recon	• ESTEEM • IDIS	• CN2 • Brute • QM	• Generator		• Recon
Decision trees			• C4.5 • C5.0		• Information Harvester	• Clementine
Dependency Relations					• TETRAD II	
Statistical Summaries	• 4Thought • Data Engine • Neural Connection	• Case Power		• Generator	• MATLAB • SAS • SPSS	• Darwin
Visualization		• Case Power	• MLC++	• Generator	• Inspect • Clementine • Recon	

Each entry within the table refers to a methodology or program lying at the intersection of two dimensions. For instance, orthogonal arrays represent a statistical technique which can be used for prediction.

Items in the table have been positioned according to their primary features. However, a particular tool may embody more than one technique or function with equal flair; in that case, it would be listed in multiple cells.

The table represents a snapshot of representative schemes and roles around the turn of the century. The two dimensions and their respective labels should remain relatively stable over the years to come.

On the other hand, the entries in any cell ought to be regarded as topical examples rather than permanent fixtures. Since techniques and applications evolve steadily, they tend to change stripes over the course of time. Without doubt, the years ahead will bring forth continuing advances in methods, software, and applications.

Agents at Work

Adaptive programs have been deployed in applications ranging from production control and economic forecasting to online shopping and virtual entertainment. An example of a learning agent is found in the Jango program. This software is the commercial version of a prototype known as ShopBot, an application developed at the University of Washington.

The agent can serve as an aide in seeking books, music, software, or other products. A number of interesting results emerged from an early experiment to verify the utility of ShopBot. The test involved an online search of the lowest price for each of four popular products, including the Word program from Microsoft and the Quicken bookkeeping package from Intuit. The human subjects in the experiment were split into three groups as follows.

A.   Individuals who used ShopBot only. On average, this group required 13 minutes and 20 seconds to find the target price for the four products.

B.   Subjects who employed only the search tools available on the Netscape browser. This group took 58 minutes and 30 seconds, on average, to find the four items.

C.   Surfers who used Netscape's search tools *and* were given the Internet addresses of 12 online vendors. This group took an average of 112 minutes and 30 seconds to find prices for all four products.

The crucial difference among the three groups lay in the time required for online search. Another notable result was the fact that the group using ShopBot usually found the lowest price for each product.

From this experiment, we may infer a number of interesting lessons. First, the ShopBot program helped users to cut their search time by three-quarters or more. Second, the agent tended to produce the best result by uncovering the lowest price. Third, information overload can ruin productivity during an online search.

The last observation derives from a comparison of the second and third groups. In particular, group C could have ignored the Internet addresses of the online stores if that information were redundant or immaterial. As a result, this band of users should have performed at least as well as group B; yet it fared much worse. *Information overload* is a term which is usually applied to executives deluged with data, but apparently it can weigh heavily on shoppers as well.

Over the past decade and more, knowledge based methods have been employed extensively in the financial sector. An example of knowledge discovery in this domain relates to credit card processing. In the United States, large issuers of cards may lose over $10 million each year due to fraud. Amidst the torrent of requests for the authorization of credit card purchases, it is a challenge to identify the rare instances of fraudulent usage. For this task, data mining tools such as neural nets have been widely employed.

The technology allows card issuers to approve transactions at once, in contrast to the pause required by a human operator. Moreover, despite the higher proportion of approved requests, the frequency of faulty authorizations is lower than that due to manual processing.

At the turn of the century, adaptive methods began to migrate in earnest into the realm of marketing. Data mining is a promising vehicle across the gamut of marketing tasks, including applications such as the following.

- Recognizing sales patterns among groups of stores.
- Discovering patterns of purchase by time of day, day of year, or type of product.
- Identifying gradual trends or abrupt shifts in customer tastes.

At a grocery store, a shopper presents his or her choices all at once at the check-out counter. The shopper's basket of goods can be analyzed for patterns among product selections. The examination of linkages among purchased products is known as *market basket analysis.* For instance, a basket analysis might yield a rule such as the following:

- A customer who buys Brand X soft drinks has a 35% chance of buying Brand Y snacks.

This kind of knowledge could be used in creating a promotional strategy for related products.

To date, applications of knowledge mining have focused largely on the analysis of data. In general, the databases contain information which is standard fare for the traditional methods of statistical analysis. The content ranges from quantitative attributes such the age of a customer to qualitative features such as the choice of a product model.

Much of human knowledge, however, is embodied in written documents including newspaper articles, corporate reports, and technical papers. The use of adept schemes for document analysis is known as *text mining,* a field which began to sprout commercial applications in the late 1990s.

In addition to the tools of machine learning, text mining relies on the techniques of language comprehension. *Natural language processing* is a multidisciplinary field which has witnessed great advances since the 1960s through the concerted work of researchers in computer science, linguistics, and cognitive psychology.

Over the past decade, practical applications of the technology have been developed in a variety of research centers around the globe. One of these, an institution funded by Xerox Corporation, is found in the Palo Alto Research Center in California. The parent company has commercialized the linguistic technology by forming a venture named Inxight Software.

Among the products marketed by Inxight, an exemplar lies in the Summarizer software. Upon the presentation of a document, the program performs a linguistic analysis, identifies key sentences, then yields a readable summary in prose.

A second program offered by Inxight Software is found in the LinguistX package. In a process known to computer scientists as *parsing*, the software identifies the basic objects and determines the grammatical role of each word in a sentence. The output can then be stored in a database of semantic relationships. The semantic database serves as the foundation for generating high-level knowledge. A sample application in this category lies in monitoring trends or predicting crises in the economy. This type of application will be examined more fully in Chapter 6.

Another tool for analyzing documents is found in the Intelligent Miner for Text, a program sold by IBM. The package can extract key information from a document or classify files into a hierarchy of topics.

Additional examples of knowledge mining in practical domains are provided in Appendices C and D. The applications range from sales forecasting and product design to online gaming and autonomous pets.

Ages of the Internet

The advent of online services during the early decades of the Internet is profiled in Table 2.2. The exhibit presents a number of popular utilities on the Net during the first stage of development.

Table 2.2. Rise of the Internet. The first generation stretched from 1968 to 1990. A sampling of services ranges from email to online dialogue.

Feature	Protocol or sample application
Electronic mail	Multipart Internet Mail Encoding
File transfer	File Transfer Protocol
Remote login	Telnet for full access to a user's privileges from a distant terminal
Multiuser conversation	Internet Relay Chat (initially for typed messages only)

During this period, the Internet was a platform built by technologists for kindred spirits. The infrastructure was originally intended for use by specialists in the scientific and military sectors. The user interfaces were atrocious, and only a technoid could love the jargon and protocols required to exploit the system.

All that changed with the release of the World Wide Web in 1991. A Web browser could provide a graphic display with an intuitive interface. At the click of a mouse, a neophyte could readily obtain articles, images, and audio clips from the far corners of the globe. The Internet turned overnight into a platform for efficiency and effectiveness for both individuals and organizations.

The World Wide Web ushered in the second generation of the Net. The new era was marked by convenient access to multimedia files, boundless content, and real-time interaction among thousands of users. A sampling of services during the second age of the Net is listed in Table 2.3.

Table 2.3. The Web in the mainstream. The second generation of the Net is slated to run from 1991 to about 2010.

Feature	Protocol or Sample Application
Hypertext	World Wide Web
Global search	Yahoo!
Virtual reality	Virtual Reality Modeling Language
Internet telephony	Voice over IP
Streaming video	RealNetworks
Multiplayer games	Everquest; Final Fantasy; Ultima Online
Broadband collaboration	Internet 2
Network computation	SETI@home
Vocal interaction	VoiceXML
Mobile media	Wireless Application Protocol; i-Mode
Portable nodes	Smart jewelry or clothes
Personal aides	Shopping agent
Extraterrestrial Web	Interplanetary Internet

The late 1990s witnessed the extension of the Internet to mobile platforms. An alliance of firms on both sides of the Atlantic introduced the Wireless Application Protocol to mediate interactions among portable phones, personal organizers, and other footloose gizmos.

Unfortunately, the protocol and its envisioned applications got off to a slow start. The tepid reception from the marketplace stemmed from the halting speed of wireless links, high cost of connections, and sparse offerings by service vendors.

Even so, the steady increase in bandwidth and the proliferation of portable devices set the stage for widespread use of mobile media. In fact, access to the Net from wireless devices was on track to exceed that from wired computers within the first few years of the millennium.

Meanwhile, on the other side of the planet, a wireless standard created in Japan became a runaway success. The i-Mode format, embraced by users and vendors alike, was to become the first major success for unwired leisure and mobile commerce.

The wirefree protocol developed in the West required a live connection to send or receive a message. The user then had to pay for the cost of the connection.

The Japanese approach, in contrast, borrowed a page from the wired Internet. As with the HyperText Transfer Protocol for tethered devices, the i-Mode employed a packet switching approach which could handle multiple streams of communication on a single channel. Moreover, the Japanese scheme enabled users to receive some types of information even when their phones were idle. Brief missives such as the notification of fresh mail could be delivered to a handset at no cost to the recipient.

Wired lines. Over the course of the 1990s, surfers in developed economies began to rely on the Net at work, school and play. The soaring demand for services was met by a rapid expansion in infrastructure. With additional capacity in place, users could access not only email and text in a jiffy, but bulkier types of files such as audio and video.

In the mid-1990s, most Netizens at home relied on telephone lines which delivered data at a speed of 14,400 bits per second (or *bps*). The capacity, or *bandwidth*, was sufficient to procure short segments of text at a moment's notice. On the other hand, longer files such as music could easily take several minutes or even hours.

Five years later, the speed had increased to 56,000 bps for most users. This was sturdy enough to enjoy Web pages with graphics, but still too limp for video.

On the other hand, an impatient surfer could subscribe to a novel method for squeezing data and pumping it down a traditional phone line. The technique, known by the generic term *Digital Subscriber Line* (DSL), could send data at rates well in excess of 1 million bps (or *Mbps*). This was enough to savor the smorgasbord of multimedia fare on the Web, including digital movies.

Unwired links. In contrast to the surge in bandwidth for wired access to the Net, unwired channels trailed about a decade behind. The 1970s had heralded the first generation of mobile phones. The handsets of that era relied on analog signals, much like the messages coursing through copper wires in a classical telephone line.

In the early days, a cellular phone was about the size and weight of a brick. Thanks to the hefty cost and bulk, handsets appealed only to niche markets such as surveyors and traveling salesmen.

The rise of digital standards led to the second generation of mobile phones in the 1990s. The new widgets came with less weight and cost, yet more features such as the ability to send snippets of text to a fellow user.

Around the turn of the century, a number of network operators offered mobile channels rated at 56,000 bps and higher. Among pioneering operators, the speed of wireless connections would roughly double every couple of years.

The arrival of the third generation in mobile technology by 2005 was destined to bring connection speeds in the ballpark of 1 Mbps and higher. Such bandwidth would be more than enough for a nomad to watch a movie on the run, or to attend a video conference in real time.

Leading edge. On the software side, the wavefront of multimedia products is driven by the entertainment sector. Applications at the bleeding edge include special effects in conventional movies and virtual worlds in online games.

Although the cutting edge of research is often found in university labs, educational users tend to trail behind in practical applications. On the other hand, the lag may shorten or even disappear in future as a result of increasing pressure for evergreen training. To avoid obsolescence, professionals in every field have to update their skills on a continuing basis. The imperative of lifelong education has opened up a vast new market. Nimble ventures have begun to tap into this market with snazzy products built on the full spectrum of multimedia capabilities.

In 1999, a large initiative was launched in the U.S. to harness the advances in hardware and software for educational environments. The project, christened Internet 2, is a consortium of universities, companies, and government agencies. The backbone of the infrastructure is a network of fiber optic cables which can carry up to 40 billion bps. The goal of the federation is to develop the second generation of utilities and applications for teaching and research.

The portfolio of projects for the consortium ranges from music lessons via online interaction to collaborative research for scientists on different continents. Other showcases span the gamut from videoconferencing via mobile widgets to privacy standards for health care centers.[10]

In 2001, the U.S. National Science Foundation initiated a project for a hypercomputer scattered across the Net. The virtual machine, officially named the Distributed Terascale Facility, connects an assortment of supercomputers at various universities and federal labs around the nation.

The name for the motley machine is derived from the capacity of existing devices. A conventional supercomputer sports a memory size of several trillion bytes, or a handful of *terabytes*. The machine can also crunch numbers at the rate of a few trillion calculations per second, or *teraflops*.[11]

The hypercomputer, known to its friends as the TeraGrid, builds on the existing fiber optic network laid out for the Internet 2 project. The pastiche of a machine is designed to address applications such as forecasting changes in climate or designing molecules for medicine.

Every moment of the day, millions of computers pass the time in idle solitude while their users forsake them for other activities. Thanks to the advent of networked computing, however, lonely machines of the world can unite in a fellowship of number crunching.

Distributed computation flared into public view with the announcement of a stellar project. For a heavenly grail, volunteers all over the globe were asked to donate idle resources on their desktop computers.

In the search for extraterrestrial intelligence (SETI), stargazers scan the heavens for signs of alien life beyond our own world. The volume of data gathered by tracking stations is so extensive, however, that it overflows the computing facilities available to astronomers.

To join the project named *SETI@home*, a volunteer first obtains a special program from a server on the Web. The program acts as a screen saver on the local computer, springing into action only when the machine is idle. After obtaining a clump of data from the central repository, the software sifts through the local batch in search of clues for intelligent life. After running the diagnostic procedures, the screen saver automatically returns the result to the central host on the Web.

By the turn of the millennium, well over two million users had downloaded and run the diagnostic program.[12] When a great society of personal computers heaves together in this fashion, the global impact is equivalent to a phalanx of supercomputers.

Speaking of intelligence in space, another project takes the Net out of this world. As spacecraft leave the Earth in increasing numbers, a flexible standard is needed to mediate communications. Probes in the field have to talk to each other and with mission control back at home. What better platform to use than the Internet: a versatile, rugged, and proven technology?

An Internet reaching across the solar system allows mission control to direct operations through a robust channel. The Net can relay not only commands and telemetry, but video scans from spacecraft flying past a comet or a rover cruising across a planet. Moreover, the general public can watch a video stream as it arrivs on Earth, without the need to fuss with the conversion of data formats.

For the first phase of deployment, the extraterrestrial Net is designed as a medium for messages between the Earth and nearby planets.[13] In the decades ahead, spacecraft will venture into deep space and cross the void betwixt the stars. The extended Net will then convey messages to and from autonomous agents in control of each vehicle and its functions.

Despite the laudable efforts of its supporters, the SETI project might fail to detect any dispatches from aliens during the first half of the 21st century. In that case, the first signs of intelligent life from the stars will come from virtual scouts on our own spacecraft as they race across the Milky Way Galaxy.

Summary

The world is in the midst of upheaval as a result of technological ferment, international trade, and cultural fusion. Against the tumult and confusion, the Internet serves as a common platform for interaction and a trusty storehouse for the wealth of information around the planet.

The open architecture of the Internet has accommodated the swift expansion of the global infobahn. From the demand side, a key attraction of the Net lies in its ability to weave a rich tapestry of data in formats ranging from text and graphics to audio and video. In particular, multimedia and virtual reality can enhance the productivity of an organization as well as its customers, suppliers, and other stakeholders.

The ubiquitous format for presenting online information lies in the HyperText Markup Language, which specifies how information is to be presented on the 2-dimensional canvas of a computer screen. A complementary standard is found in the Java programming language. This standard is a general-purpose language which can be used to depict objects within an HTML document or control other objects on a network. For instance, an applet written in Java might be used to animate a dog in a 2-D scene whose overall structure is specified in HTML. In an analogous way, Java can be used to process information or specify complex relationships among objects in a 3-D world.

Multimedia systems can convey information more quickly than solitary channels such as text or voice alone. Moreover, cyberspace offers instant access to a global market at negligible marginal cost. With the expansion of wireless services, the growth of dataland will proceed even faster in the years to come.

In conjunction with Internet technologies, smart software can generate useful knowledge from raw data in any realm. Adept agents draw on the data mining techniques of statistics, graphic media, and machine learning.

To an increasing extent, adaptive schemes will be employed in every field where records have to be analyzed for conceptual modeling, synthesized into express knowledge, or transformed into practical action. The types of functions which can be automated include the following.

- Procuring information
- Analyzing data
- Automating routine
- Discovering patterns
- Predicting outcomes

At the forefront of data mining lie hybrid schemes which incorporate several primal techniques. The effectiveness of compound methods has been demonstrated in areas ranging from product configuration and customer service to portfolio management and economic forecasting.

The first generation of the Net spanned the period from 1968 to 1990. This era witnessed the rise of basic communications, ranging from electronic mail and file transfer to remote access and typed dialogue.

With the release of the World Wide Web in 1991, the Internet was poised to enter the daily routine. The second generation has brought a cascade of multimedia applications, from streaming video and virtual reality to personal agents and mobile games.

Wireless channels and smart media in cyberland provide the foundations for a second industrial revolution. The technologies have begun to permeate the panoply of human activity. In due course, the increase in creativity and productivity will energize the next stage of cultural evolution.

Chapter 3

Pioneers on the Web

A key to prosperity in the age of knowledge is a robust groundwork for information and communication. The failure of the former Soviet Union has driven home the message that a rich cultural heritage and a vast scientific base will not by themselves ensure economic success.

Squelching the flow of information from diverse sectors of the economy ended up throttling the wealth of resources available to the Soviets. For certain industries such as oil production, the processed output was in fact less valuable in the global marketplace than the raw material used as input. Perhaps this more than any other aspect highlights the sorry consequences of ignoring or mishandling information.

In advanced economies, the majority of national income is derived from services of various kinds, ranging from travel and banking to leisure and education. The engine of the service sector is information: its collection, dissemination, and exploitation.

Data processing constitutes not only the backbone of a healthy economy, but a significant sector on its own. Digital technology comprises a global market whose yearly revenues hover in the neighborhood of a trillion dollars. A country with serious plans to tap into this market must itself be an innovator and experienced user of digital products.

The sphere of influence for informatics extends beyond the marketplace. In a modern society, computation is a foundation for competence in every domain, ranging from scientific research and product design to logistic planning and financial activity. In each of these spheres, an economy or an organization without a proper digital infrastructure can only be, at best, a second-rate operation.

At the dawn of the 20th century, the United States was still a developing country with an emerging internal market. By the 1940s, however, the nation had become the undisputed champion of the world economy. Within half a century, the U.S. had transformed itself from a largely agrarian economy into the leading industrial power on the planet.

By the turn of the millennium, the U.S. had again positioned itself at the forefront of an emerging market. The nation today serves as the wellspring of innovation and the vanguard of the charge into the digital economy.

A Tale of Two Regions

Two renowned areas of innovation lie within the Route 128 corridor in Massachusetts and Silicon Valley in California. In 1959, Route 128 dominated the technology landscape in America, with 268 firms employing a total of 61,409 persons. In contrast, the same year saw only 109 firms in Silicon Valley employing 17,376 individuals.[14]

By 1975, however, total employment in the Valley exceeded that of Route 128. The steady ascent of the Valley continued in the subsequent decades. By 1992, the Valley employed 249,259 people in 4,063 technology firms as opposed to 140,643 people in 2,513 companies around Route 128.

A number of factors have been identified for the success of Silicon Valley.

●   *Networking.* The Valley is densely populated with small and medium enterprises which interact closely. On the other hand, Route 128 has been dominated by large, vertically integrated firms such as Raytheon and the former Digital Equipment Corporation; employees in the Northeast seldom interact with those in other companies.

●   *Technology transfer.* Numerous technologies are conceived in university labs, then nurtured by industrial concerns. Since World War II, Stanford University has actively encouraged local start-ups. In contrast, MIT has tended to remain aloof from venture activities.

●   *Attitude toward failure.* In the Valley, failure is regarded as a stepping stone to success. After having failed, an entrepreneur has no difficulty in starting another venture or finding employment with a going concern. On the other hand, the tradition-bound culture of the East Coast stigmatizes failure. Creativity in any discipline is a risky affair: each success is built on a heap of failures. For this reason, fear of flops is a crushing burden on the practice of innovation.

No doubt the centuries of heritage and the resulting conservatism are major hurdles to innovation in New England. Presumably the rain and snow also contribute to the relative isolation of both organizations and individuals within the coziness of their own walls.

The first two factors in the preceding checklist appear to be directly manipulable by governments, universities, and companies. For instance, public agencies can encourage industry consortia or award research and development projects to upstart firms. In addition, universities can promote technology transfer by providing proper incentives for the collaboration of faculty and entrepreneurs.

Cultural factors such as the attitude toward failure possess great inertia and do not shift overnight. But even here, change can be catalyzed by design. For instance, research grants may be awarded on the merits of an idea regardless of the prior business history of the applicant. As another example, the media can publicize the successes of individuals who have surmounted formidable obstacles, including repeated failures along the way. By such means, invention and venturing can be promoted as a standard path for all comers rather than a wild aberration for iconoclasts.

World at the Screen

Information technologies provide an economy with the means to accelerate or circumvent entire stages of industrial development. At the onset of the 21st century, only a hallucinator would rank India as an industrial power. While the country has a respectable manufacturing capability, the industrial sector comprises only a small part of the overall economy.

Even so, a number of firms in India are the main suppliers of commercial software for numerous firms in advanced economies. Efficient channels of communication allow programmers on the subcontinent to work half a world away from their customers. The pay scale for these software developers is modest by Western standards; but more to the point, the wages are generous in comparison to other workers in India.

An example of distributed processing which is even more prevalent around the globe is found in back office operations. Record-keeping activities for airlines, banks, and other firms in the West are often provided in real time by overseas partners working in the Philippines,

Ireland, or other countries on the periphery of the major economic regions.

These are examples of functions where developing economies act as suppliers to Western customers. The same technologies of the Net enable a local vendor to market his own products to the world at large.

The fastest-growing market today is found in cyberspace, where myriads of potential customers peruse the far-flung nodes of the online realm. And within the Net, the swiftest expansion is taking place in the dynamic forum known as the World Wide Web. The Web offers convenient access to products and services as well as facts and figures, news and ideas.

Mature firms such as AT&T display their wares on the Web, jostling with brash startups which have yet to outgrow the kitchen table. For a modest investment in hardware and software, the same technology allows an artisan in Malaysia to offer her products with similar speed and flair. With the technology, a merchant can communicate with a customer on the far side of the globe with as much convenience as a client on the other side of town.

The Web is also a colorful window into a virtual library with vast holdings around the world. A sociologist in rural Brazil can obtain the latest article from an archive in California with the same ease that a programmer in Indonesia can download the spiffiest tool from a software institute in Germany. For many types of information access, the personal cost of using the system tends to be uniformly low: often zilch.

This chapter presents a survey of the digital terrain during the first wave of expansion into dataland. It displays the main outcrops in the landscape and profiles examples of pioneering ventures.

Thanks to the tempo of advances in the field, many of the original firms on the Web have already metamorphosed. A number of ventures have merged, others gone bankrupt and yet others revamped their mission.

Although the scenery will continue to change in the details, the large-scale panorama will endure somewhat longer. For this reason, the generic concepts presented in this chapter should remain valid for years to come, if not decades.

Paradox of All and None

As with any untrodden terrain, the world of the virtual presents its surprises. Perhaps the most remarkable facet lies in the comfortable mixture of everything and nothing.

Along the zero direction, the Internet offers a frictionless way to conduct business. The marginal cost of operation is practically nil, while the response time for user interactions can be negligible. To illustrate, a large program may be expensive to construct, but once deployed it may be replicated at trivial cost.

In the opposite direction, the Net in some ways knows no limits. Cyberspace offers a boundless cache of data, know-how, and entertainment. Moreover, an individual or firm with a Web page can reach out at once to a global audience which in a previous age had been accessible only at great expense.

In the middling ground between everything and nothing, the technology of the infosphere presents innumerable opportunities for enterprising ventures. For instance, the volume of information throughout cyberia has engendered digital guides to advise both rookies and veterans of virtual gems in the realm.

An *infomediary* is an intermediary which sells information about an online market, or provides a platform for transactions between buyers and sellers. The virtual facilitator may cater to individuals or organizations.

In particular, a retail mediator offers a service for consumers. The first generation of mediators is typified by portals into cyberspace, the most visible of which is found in Yahoo. Other infomediaries are merchants such as Amazon, or auction services such as eBay.

On the other hand, a wholesale infomediary provides a service for an organization. These enterprises might be regarded as the second generation of infomediaries.

An example lies in Adauction, which sells advertising space at a discount. Another instance is found in the National Transportation Exchange: the broker provides a match between users of freight space and trucking firms, whose vehicles often travel empty-handed on their return trips.

The wholesale market – also known as *business-to-business*, or *B2B* – enjoys munificent revenues in dataland. In the U.S. alone, this market was slated to reach trillions of dollars within the first few years of the century.[15] The commission on transactions, at an average fee of 5%, comes to a plush penny. From the transaction fees, gross margins are estimated to be roughly 85%.[16]

Cyberspace offers visions of untold wealth in a virgin land which stretches to the ends of time and space. With this allure, the digital frontier has attracted a gaggle of earnest prospectors as well as gold diggers. The seekers of opportunity range from technologists and visionaries to merchants and charlatans.

No doubt digitopia will offer up its treasures in due course. In the short run, however, cyberland has often been coy about revealing its virtual bounties.

One reason for the difficulty of earning a living in bitville springs from its heritage of asking for nothing. This liberal tradition is bound up in the culture of the original trekkers to cyberland.

Culture of the Free

Individual scientists may be driven by personal devils, including greed, power and passion. On the other hand, the scientific fraternity as a whole is energized by nobler motives such as the quest for knowledge and contribution to society. In this milieu, much knowledge and effort is donated freely to the community at large.

As explained in Chapter 2, the origins of the Internet lie in defense-related research. For decades afterward, however, the Net served as a collaborative vehicle for researchers around the planet. Given this lineage, cyberspace has retained the ethos of societal service even to this day. In particular, the planetary Web is a vast storehouse of facts, knowledge, and programs which are often provided at little or no cost to the user.

A product which is offered without any strings – nor warranties – is called *freeware*. This type of item is at times confused with *shareware*: a commercial product which a user may try out for free, but is expected to submit a nominal fee should the program be exploited in earnest.

Many sites on the Net provide links to both freeware and shareware. One source which specializes in the distribution of digital products is Download.com. The enterprise features software goodies of all kinds, and covers its costs primarily from corporate sponsors.

A multitude of firms on the Web offers services at little or no cost to the user. To illustrate, anyone can become an entrepreneur without incurring a financial burden. For this purpose, a firm named Vstore provides a personal storefront for free to any Netizen. To set up shop, a user first decides on the type of product to sell, be it books, sneakers, or some other category. Next, the would-be owner chooses a store template from the selection on display at Vstore. The proprietor then selects the models to feature at his site, choosing from a stockpile of millions of items from allied vendors.

On a trip to the shopowner's Website, an errant visitor might decide to order a product or three. For the retail transaction, Vstore handles all the back office activities, from order acceptance to customer service. After the sale is completed, the shopowner receives a commission of 5 to 25%, depending on the product.

Cyberspace also offers the means to create an online community without incurring any financial risk. An enterprise in this vein is found in Outblaze, an operator of Web services. Although the firm was established in 1998 in Hong Kong, its hardware servers are located in the U.S. The "Instant Portal" is a free communal service offered by the firm; with this arrangement, a client acquires a virtual portal on computers maintained by Outblaze. Free services for the associate include a chat room and message board, plus email accounts for members of the new portal. In return, the guest organization shares its membership list and advertising revenues with Outblaze.

Revenue Models

The Net harbors a profusion of resources in the form of data, software, and services. Moreover, many of its wares are free for the asking. While the freewheeling culture is a bonanza for consumers, it is a bugbear for vendors.

During the first wave of mass migration to cyberia, most online ventures were bottomless sinks for funds. Investors poured billions of dollars into profitless firms in the faith that some day the long streak of red ink would chart a path to a fountain of wealth.

With a conviction bordering on religion, many entrepreneurs sought to mine the uncharted fields of the Net. After numerous forays, a fortunate few began to strike gold in the late 1990s. Experience since then has yielded a handful of revenue models, ranging from advertising premiums and subscription fees to transaction fees and software rental.

Advertising. Over the next decade or two, advertising on the Net will soar even faster than the expanding base of surfers. In 1999, online advertising in the U.S. amounted to $3.3 billion; this figure represented 3% of total ad expenditures.

Other parts of the world lagged the U.S. in digital marketing. For instance, virtual ads in Asia amounted to $237 million in 1999, representing 1% of total advertising in the region.[17] On the other hand, online advertising was estimated at the better part of a trillion U.S. dollars in 2000, and double that for the following year.

A prime beneficiary of the growth in advertising is found in Yahoo, a search engine for the Web. The firm enjoys a profit rate in the neighborhood of 30% on revenues.

At the century's turn, online ads were confined largely to notices on the periphery of the user interface. To an increasing degree, ads will pop up as a matter of course in the nooks and crannies of virtual worlds. An example of such advertising lies in a jingle for Coca Cola on the radio as the user drives along a simulated road in his virtual Jaguar.

Subscription fees. Entertainment is a prime attraction in cyberspace. Bandai, the Japanese creator of the Tamagotchi game, offers cartoons from its Website. The service is accessible with a subscription fee of about US$1 each month.

Encyclopaedia Britannica offers its namesake product for sale as packaged software on a compact disk. The firm also provides similar content on the Net, together with additional resources. An enhanced service on the Web, including continual updates to the information on the CD, is offered for $50 per year.

Software rental. For much of its history, computer software was either leased, purchased, or procured for free. With any of these mechanisms, a copy of the program resided on a local computer. In fact, the status of personal computers as islands of computation could not support any other means of software deployment.

This model of computation began to dissolve in the 1980s as organizations shed their support functions, ranging from accounting and tracking to payroll and distribution. When a peripheral function was relegated to an external contractor, the latter would assume complete responsibility for processing the data.

An intermediate arrangement appeared in the late 90s. With the new approach, software was rented on the run by the client enterprise. The customer would then pay a nominal fee for each invocation of the program.

The rental of software was championed in its early stages by BizTone, a provider of business services on the Net. The firm began offering its products in May 1999, based on programs written in the Java language.

Software rental is in tune with a larger trend which has been in progress for decades in the United States; namely, bolstering competitive advantage by focusing on a core set of skills. As a corollary, the enterprise sheds non-critical functions ranging from manufacturing to accounting. Why invest in facilities for an ancillary task when the operation can be outsourced? As a result of the secular trend toward streamlining, the rental model is likely to enjoy steady growth in the years ahead.

Transaction fees. A transaction fee is a commission for facilitating a commercial operation. On the Net, a premium for mediation is often derived by hosting a service of some kind.

One popular vehicle lies in an auction at either the retail or wholesale level. An example of a successful auctioneer catering to consumers is found in the popular site known as eBay.

A wholesale auction, on the other hand, supports business-to-business activities. A veteran in this category is found in Freemarket.com. Even by 1998, the firm had hosted annual sales in excess of $1 billion.

Another type of service relying on transaction fees takes the form of purchasing groups. A buying pool comprises a group of individuals or firms banding together to obtain volume discounts. The participants can then place orders jointly or separately.

An example of a buyer pool is PurchasingCenter.com. The consortium handles industrial goods such as wires, tapes, and tools. In the virtual alliance, firms which huddle together can expect savings of 10 to 15%. Meanwhile, a buyer that uses the central Website to issue multiple bids can expect to save roughly 20%. The PurchasingCenter collects a fee of 4% or so, depending on the type of transaction.

Premium fees. A revenue model which is increasing in popularity takes the form of samples or enticements: certain items are free, and others not. In a typical arrangement, a basic set of products is offered with no strings attached. These products serve as *loss leaders* in the hope that users will subsequently move up to higher-quality services at a premium.

A case in point lies with Bigstep.com, a provider of free Websites for online ventures. Founded in 1998, the firm targets small businesses. In 1999, less than 10% of over 7 million small businesses in the U.S. had Websites. Within a few years, a presence in cyberspace was de rigueur even for small fry such as pizza parlors.

Bigstep provides basic services without charge. For instance, a firm named Apex might obtain a unique domain name such as apex.bigstep.com. The Website can then be molded as desired by the client firm. The hosting service provides tools for managing customers, the likes of which include a program to maintain a customer database or a utility to issue newsletters by email. Other templates include an electronic catalog or portfolio to display products, as well as software to analyze traffic at the client's Website.

Guest firms requiring expanded services are assessed a nominal fee. For example, a client enterprise might decide to accept credit card payments from customers. Bigstep provides such services for a mixed fee: $14.95 each month plus 15 cents per transaction in addition to a discount rate of 2.67% on the credit card purchase.

Professional services of all types will continue to proliferate on the Net. These range from virtual portals for corporate treasurers to online markets for freelance programmers.

Payment by phone. The explosive growth of mobile gadgets offers a convenient vehicle for marketing. Throughout the 1990s, the personal computer was the standard device for accessing the Net. In many localities, this role is being usurped by wireless devices such as smartphones.

For marketers, the shift in channels is a welcome development. Since phone customers have an ingrained habit of paying merely for connection time – let alone obtaining value-added services – mobile devices represent an attractive platform for marketing products at a sustainable price.

A pioneer in the practice of charging by phone is found in Sonera, the largest cellular operator in Finland. A customer may use his smartphone to order a drink from a vending machine, as well as purchase golf balls or car washes. The expense is tallied and presented together with the subscriber's regular phone bill at the end of the month.

Another wireless marketer lies in WapIT, a content provider for mobile phones. The firm works in collaboration with Radiolinja of Finland and Hewlett-Packard of the U.S. WapIt offers hundreds of services ranging from news and horoscopes to blind dating and anonymous chat rooms.

Through long experience, phone users are psychologically prepared to pay for products and services in connection with their phone bill. Moreover, access to the Net through mobile gizmos is overtaking links from wired devices. For these reasons, unwired marketing is becoming the channel of choice for all types of vendors in the digital economy.

Knowledge as Property

In the age of electronica, the ease of replicating virtual products threatens traditional modes of distribution. For instance, a music file can be copied at will in the absence of security mechanisms to prevent duplication.

If a product can be replicated without paying dues to its creator, the financial incentive for innovation crumbles. Although some individuals would continue to create beautiful music out of intrinsic pleasure, the volume of output would surely decline. (Of course, some might welcome a fall in volume as a positive development, but this view is not universally shared.)

One mechanism for protecting digital content is found in a software container from IBM. The Cryptolope, or *cryto*graphic enve*lope*, is a digital box which reveals its contents only upon presentation of the correct key.

An alternate tool for digital protection is found in the Commerce Modeler from a firm named Intertrust. With this system, a publisher can set usage rights and pricing policy for each digital piece. For instance, the vendor can offer a discounted price for a song if the buyer purchases a ticket for a related concert at the same time.

Another vehicle for securing digital documents comes from an enterprise known as PublishOne. The company operates computers, known as file servers, which disseminate documents contributed by participating authors and publishing firms. The contributor of each file determines the permissible actions and their attendant fees. For instance, a buyer may print or copy a particular file twice by paying the proper fee at the outset.

When PublishOne receives a document from its owner, the file is wrapped in a digital container and presented on the Website of a marketing partner. After registering with a financial mediator, a purchaser may download the proper software to open the container.

An example of a hardware solution to the problem of digital protection lies in the Copyright chip by Wave Systems. With this approach, the hardware for encoding a document is embedded in the chipset of a PC. Since the encoding is hardwired, the system is impervious to tampering by software hackers.

The proper scope for digital rights management is hotly contested by vendors who argue that more is better, and liberal spirits who claim that less is more. The years to come will see numerous schemes to secure digital products, and others to untie them. Against this background, a long string of battles is likely to erupt in the courts before a suitable agreement is reached by a concord of users, vendors, and regulators.

Harvesting a Venture

For many digital entrepreneurs, the holy grail lies in a stock market listing. To this end, a variety of services have sprouted in cyberia to assist a venture on its journey to an initial public offering (IPO). Through these agents, private investors can also purchase IPO shares directly on the Net.

The leading contenders among the new class of merchant bankers include the Wit Capital Group. One of the minority shareholders in Wit is the venerable firm of Goldman Sachs. Another example of a digital banker is found in E*Offering, which distributes IPO's to customers of the online broker named E*Trade.

Yet other firms provide background information on the IPO scene. Examples of such firms are found in IPO.com or the IPO Financial Network.

Giants in cyberspace. Although virtual commerce is in its infancy, it has already given birth to sprawling giants. A heavyweight in this category takes the form of Softbank Corporation.

The firm was established in 1981 by Masayoshi Son as a vehicle for distributing software products in Japan. In 1995, the corporation established a subsidiary, Softbank Technology Ventures, to focus on investment opportunities in Internet services. Between 1995 and 1998,

Softbank and its subsidiaries purchased 72% of Yahoo, whose pretax margin in 1998 was 21%.

In 1996 Softbank established Yahoo Japan, with 51% ownership. Two years later the restless player bought 27% of the online brokerage E*Trade for $400 million; the value of this holding would balloon to $2.4 billion within a year. By 1999, Softbank and its venture division had invested $1.7 billion in more than 100 Net companies, thereby securing a dominant position in the virtual economy.

In addition to a few giants, the digital revolution spawned an ecosystem of fledgling firms during the first wave of euphoria. Many of the enterprises, backed more by hype than substance, collapsed when the speculative bubble burst in spring 2000. Thanks to the pop, the runaway fever subsided before reaching dangerous levels.

A saner environment came to prevail in the aftermath. To last the course, a virtual ventures would now have to embrace meaningful goals as well as technical skills and managerial savvy. In this aspect, at least, an enterprise in bitville was to be no different from one in rockland.

Expanding Directions

The advent of broadband capabilities on wireless links has unleashed the Net from its tethers. The years ahead will draw forth a lively circus of active media and clever products in cyberspace.

In digitopia, basic services such as Net access or file storage have become commodity products with low profit margins. For this reason, attractive opportunities have receded to the high ground of value-added services. A sample application in this category is found in real-time synopses of news articles. Another specimen lies in the automatic extraction of helpful knowledge from databases by the use of data mining techniques.

To ensure success, a firm has to polish its core skills and fashion a strategic plan which takes into account the economics of virtual competition. A systematic approach to crafting a corporate strategy is the subject of Chapter 5.

Summary

To join the ranks of leadership in the age of knowledge, a nation has to establish itself in the technologies of information. For this mission, the critical role for a government is to ensure online access, nurture technical innovation, and promote digital entrepreneurship.

The diffusion of know-how across national borders and the consequent erosion of profits applies to products lines as well as entire industries. In the early 1990s, Toyota enjoyed a gross margin of thousands of dollars on each vehicle it shipped. By the turn of the century, however, the carmaker earned only a fraction of its former margins. For a number of global firms such as Toyota, the astute management of foreign exchange transactions occasionally contributed to a larger fraction of corporate profits than did the earnings from traditional lines of business.

The informatic arena is marked by the same trends of technology diffusion and profit erosion. The production of memory chips, which embody less technical content than microprocessors, migrated from the U.S. to Japan in the 1980s, and subsequently to Korea and Taiwan. Having become largely a commodity product, the storage chip offers lower margins than a logic processor. In fact, memory chips have already begun their exodus from their second generation of host countries to nations lower on the scale of technical development.

Digital competence is the path to competitive advantage for a firm as well as economic growth for a country in general. The strength of the commercial sector ultimately translates into a higher standard of living and the economic security of a nation.

Information is the lifeblood of a modern society. For this reason, developing regions cannot afford to be left behind in the backwaters of the knowledge economy. If emerging nations are to keep up with – and, in the longer run, match – the prosperity of the progressive countries, they have little choice but to rally to the flag of cyberia. To this end, the technologist, entrepreneur, and statesman have to find common ground from which to launch an orderly expansion across the digital divide.

Chapter 4

Managing the Virtual

At the dawn of the 21st century, the world of business is in the midst of a metamorphosis. To keep pace with the changes, firms of all types are converting themselves into virtual enterprises to better manage relations among all stakeholders: customers, employees, suppliers, regulators, and even rivals.

The main drivers behind the changeover stem from the globalization of markets in parallel with advances in informatics – in particular, computation, communications, and knowledge management. Brisk progress has produced a steady stream of digital tools and competitive tactics in the virtual arena.

Along with the proliferation of the Internet, the move to cyberia is prompted by advances in interactive media as well as savvy software. This chapter explores the core techniques, emerging trends, and resulting changes in managerial practice.

Fuzzy Frontier

The weightless economy weighs heavily on an executive. The decision maker confronts a bewildering array of new-fangled techniques, aggressive players, and punishing scuffles in global markets.

Thanks to the tumult, the sureties of yesteryear splinter into the uncertainties of the morrow. Despite the murkiness, however, the manager is vaguely aware of the need to resolve a gamut of issues such as the following.

- Taking advantage of global markets enabled by Internet commerce. For instance, a corporate Website has to experiment continually with new services for visitors while ensuring the timeliness of information and the security of transactions.

- Harnessing the forces of decentralization to fortify the competitiveness of the enterprise. An example is found in the practice of outsourcing the manufacturing and accounting functions while retaining design and marketing in-house.

- Managing the trend toward centralization, such as mergers to promote efficiency and synergism. Some high-profile marriages from the 1990s include Citicorp and Travelers Group in financial services, or Daimler and Chrysler in automobiles.

- Grappling with the advantages and pitfalls of alliances to respond to turbulent markets. A sample is found in joint ventures to accelerate time to market with breakthrough products.

- Leveraging the impact of multimedia communications on corporate productivity. A case in point lies in slashing travel time through video conferencing, or pruning the cost of training via online programs.

- Motivating workers in a business environment where lifetime employment is an anachronism. One retentive measure to promote loyalty takes the form of stock options. Another incentive is to offer professional training to enhance the long-term employability of workers, regardless of their career paths which might weave across multiple companies.

Even in the millennium, the ultimate mission of an enterprise will surely stand: contributing to societal welfare by delighting customers, rewarding shareholders, and nurturing employees. Unfortunately, as a result of jolting changes in technologies and markets, the path to the goal is difficult to discern, let alone the vehicles to reach the objective.

On the other hand, it is also clear that a paralysis of decision making—or even mere hesitation—is an invitation to organizational collapse. Only proactive maneuvering will ensure the long term survival of an enterprise.

The quickening tempo of business underscores the need to deploy advanced systems to secure competitive advantage. An informatic system should take full advantage of virtual capabilities, both within the firm and in relation to external partners including customers and suppliers. The architecture has to incorporate data warehousing and knowledge mining techniques as well as multimedia tools to support managerial analysis.

The technologies of cyberland – including network standards, multimedia, and smart agents – were presented in Chapter 2. For this reason, the discussion here will focus on managerial issues rather than technical aspects.

Explosion of Online Commerce

The march to cyberspace turned into a rush at the end of the previous century. Until the advent of the Web in 1991, the Internet had been the sole turf of a small band of technical folks. By 1999, however, 160 million individuals around the world were regular surfers.

Although digital commerce was a relative novelty, business was also expanding at a sizzling rate. According to a survey of respondents in 27 countries, the fraction of corporate revenues in 2000 attributed to a presence on the Internet was 4.7%. The estimate for the following year doubled to 9.5% as organizations around the globe stepped up their advance into cyberspace.[18]

In 2000, 36 million consumers spent about US$300 on average to generate retail sales of $10.8 billion in cyberia.[19] This was a small fraction of the $657 billion in worldwide revenues via electronic commerce for both the retail and wholesale sectors that year.[20]

More to the point for managers everywhere, online transactions were exploding at an exponential rate. The level of ecommerce around the globe was on track to nearly double each year over the intermediate term. At that rate of growth, Internet commerce would comprise the majority of the gross world product by the second half of the decade.

An interesting trend in digital business relates to the demographics of consumers. During its early phase, digitopia attracted primarily the upper echelons of the economic strata. In 1998, households earning over $50,000 accounted for 47% of the total retail segment of the economy; yet their share of online sales was disproportionately large, at 74%.

On the other hand, excursions into cyberspace by lower income groups were expanding faster than trips from the wealthier ranks. As a result, households earning less than $50,000 were destined to comprise the minority of online sales by the turn of the century.

In addition to the exploding volume of transactions, the Internet has spawned novel business practices across the board from design and marketing to pricing and distribution. The flexibility of the digital marketplace is reflected in *dynamic pricing*, where the cost of a product can vary from one moment to the next. Changes in price may be effected in real time by the vendor or customer, whether acting independently or collectively.

To illustrate, the price of a soda at a vending machine might be determined by an internal program which takes into account the time of day, season of year, level of inventory, and pattern of demand. On the other hand, a change in price may also be initiated by a bidder, as in the case of a buyer at an auction.

A service provider which caters to the demand side of the marketplace is found in Priceline.com. The firm collects bids from individual customers, then aggregates the orders to negotiate discounts with vendors ranging from airlines to hotels.

Retail Functions

The Web provides a convenient platform for customers as a result of its multimedia capabilities and 24-hour availability. For vendors, cyberspace offers a complementary set of advantages. First, online marketing establishes a storefront to the entire world. Second, a Website requires low cost compared to television or other traditional media. Third, the global network offers a high-growth channel for distribution.

Sales activity on the Web can be handled through packaged software. A program designed for customer relationship management (CRM) may serve as a front-end module to handle queries from visitors or to recognize the profiles of promising prospects. Meanwhile, an enterprise resource planning (ERP) package can support routine transactions across the entire firm, from order processing to work scheduling and product distribution.

One type of software for customer interaction lies in a tracking program to monitor a user's activities during a visit to a Website. A sample program in this category is found in Aria, a product marketed by a software vendor named Macromedia. The functions in the program include the ability to monitor the navigation path taken by a visitor to the Website. Another function in Aria identifies the domain of the visitor, his browser type, and so on. The information can be used by a marketer to profile the behavior of customers in general as well as issue messages tailored to a particular visitor.

Keeping a Tight Rein

A major corporation usually deals with a world-wide network of suppliers, warehouses, distributors, and retailers. Through this network of relationships, raw materials are procured, transformed into products, delivered to customers, and maintained after sale.

The cycle time for order fulfillment covers the period from the arrival of an order to the delivery of the finished good. The process involves the coordination of diverse activities including sales commitment, credit approval, production, and logistics.

An exemplar of supply chain integration is found at Dell Computer, a firm which derives its revenues largely through the Net. Thanks to the corporate extranet, a customer can access Dell's entire supply chain.

At the other end, the suppliers have real-time access to Dell's database of customer orders. As a result, it is a simple matter to track a package from the factory to the buyer's doorstep. In this way, both Dell and its customers can save on the costs of phone and fax queries.

Another virtuoso of the virtual is found in Cisco Systems, a vendor of networking devices such as Internet routers. Of the firm's revenues of about $10 billion in 1999, three-quarters were generated through its Website. When customers select products from the online catalog, over half of all orders pass through Cisco - without human intervention - to production facilities run by contract manufacturers. Moreover, 80% of queries from customers and partners are answered through the Net.

Cisco utilizes the Web for procurement, recruiting and other functions. For instance, travel reports and other forms are processed online. The corporate intranet also handles employee benefits, including sales of stock.

Thanks to its Web facilities, Cisco reportedly saved over $500 million even in the initial stage of online implementation. Partly as a result, the firm enjoyed a profit rate of about 35% on revenues in 1999.

A popular theory during the late 90s was that trendy outfits could prosper purely in bitspace, without tatty ties to dusty turf. Experience over the years has blunted enthusiasm for this view, at least where physical goods are concerned. The turn of the century brought a new conviction that atoms and bits need to coexist.

The paradigm of *multichannel retailing* refers to the integrated distribution of products through the Net in parallel with traditional channels such as physical stores or paper catalogues. In the unified approach, brick sites are often used to sign up customers and handle problems such as returning a product.

A deft practitioner of multichannel marketing is found in Charles Schwab, a brokerage service. About two-thirds of the firm's customers are recruited through physical offices; subsequently, the clients conduct most of their transactions online.

Another exemplar of integrated marketing is Gateway, a vendor of computer hardware. Prospective customers can "test drive" computer hardware in physical shops. Since the stores carry little inventory, however, buyers are obliged to place orders for future delivery.

Database Marketing

The Web provides a convenient vehicle for customizing services. This function is the domain of database marketing, which tailors a promotion based on a collection of customer profiles and purchase histories. To this end, smart software can be deployed as automated tools to discover knowledge, and as aides to support human deliberation.

Database marketing has been deployed in a sporadic fashion for decades. Only in the late 90s, however, did the field begin to attain a high profile within the enterprise. The ascent of database marketing during this period resulted from a variety of developments.

One factor lay in the proliferation of databases due to the declining cost of collecting and storing data. This was coupled with a growing conviction that the archives contain latent value. Within a single enterprise, the ragtag collection of databases scattered across diverse departments was consolidated. The result was a digital warehouse to ensure convenient access for all decision makers. The integrated repository provided the basis for assessing strategies and deploying resources to match shifting conditions in the environment.

To take full advantage of the information in a digital warehouse, adaptive programs have been applied to a wide range of functions. As noted earlier, the role of data mining is to discover patterns, trends or relations in databases.[21]

The automated approach to knowledge discovery is especially useful when dealing with large data sets or complex relationships. For many applications, automated software may find subtle patterns which escape the notice of manual analysis, or whose complexity exceeds the cognitive abilities of humans. Secondly, nimble software makes it feasible to analyze large data sets which would require an unjustifiable amount of manual effort. Lastly, automated tools may monitor complex domains such as global logistics on a continuous basis, then react immediately to the outbreak of new developments.

An illustrative application of knowledge mining lies in the discovery of generic patterns of behavior among consumers. The purpose of *market segmentation* is to classify potential or actual customers into distinct clusters consisting of individuals, groups, or organizations having similar needs. A typical market segment is characterized by factors such as geography, product requirements, and mode of usage. Other attributes include demographics such as age and gender as well as psychographics including personality, motivation, and lifestyle.

A related task in marketing is the analysis of purchasing behavior by a particular customer. Knowledge mining can be used to predict the response of an individual to different forms of advertising, ranging from television and radio to magazines and Websites.

An array of learning schemes is presented in Table 4.1. The chart lists a variety of techniques in concert with a sampling of their applications. For instance, case based reasoning (CBR) may be applied to tasks such as the classification of designs, the configuration of networks, and the resolution of requests.

Table 4.1. Examples of data mining applications in commerce.

- ■ Neural network
  - Market segmentation
  - Forecasting sales levels based on shipments
  - Identification of product families
- ■ Case based reasoning
  - Grouping of product designs
  - Configuration of distribution networks
  - Responding to queries from potential customers
- ■ Induction
  - Customer segmentation
  - Recognition of crucial features in a product
  - Trend forecasting
- ■ Genetic algorithm
  - Resource optimization
  - Distribution scheduling
  - Logistics planning
- ■ Statistics
  - Clustering of product groups
  - Forecasting production requirements
  - Feature selection through experimental designs
- ■ Multistrategy methods
  - Synthesis of advertising strategies
  - Improvement of scheduling plans
  - Visual exploration of data sets
  - Prediction of complex processes

Knowing Your Customer

Thanks to the Web, cyberspace has become a sizable component of the economic landscape. Despite the increasing role of online transactions, however, relatively little was known about the patterns of usage and purchasing on the Web during the formative years.

To date, a variety of online surveys have been conducted and the resulting data analyzed through statistical techniques such as multiple regression. However, due to the inherent complexity of consumer behavior, adaptive techniques from the field of artificial intelligence can yield better performance in analytic tasks, including models of online behavior.

This section illustrates the use of data mining through a case study in predicting consumer behavior. In particular, the performance of neural nets and case based reasoning is compared against the standard statistical method of linear regression. The objective is to forecast the extent of online purchases through the Web.

As indicated in Chapter 2, a neural net offers many advantages such as robustness and graceful degradation.[22] However, the procedure is hampered by a few constraints such as the sluggish rate of learning. Another drawback lies in the implicit nature of the acquired knowledge, which is difficult for a human to fathom.[23]

On the other hand, case based reasoning offers the advantage of working with data in their original format. Often the methodology is effective even when applied to an incomplete or partially faulty database.

Meanwhile, statistical techniques represent a long-standing approach to acquiring insight into the nature of data.[24] As it happens, statistical schemes such as regression, factor analysis, and other methods tend to focus on straightforward relationships which can be described through the equations of linear algebra. The nature of a linear linkage is illustrated by a worker who produces twice as many widgets each month due to a doubling of his working hours. In this example, productive output is directly proportional to the level of input.

On the other hand, the real world is rife with nonlinear relationships. For instance, a salesman who is already chugging along at 90 hours a week cannot double his working hours under any circumstances, since a week has only 168 hours.

Another example of a nonlinear phenomenon is found in a financial crash. Most of the time, a market index vacillates within a narrow hand, constrained by a rough balance of optimism and pessimism among investors. One item of moderately bad news will not shake the market's confidence; nor will two nor five. Yet a succession of bad news will at some point shatter the market's equilibrium, and trigger a sudden plunge in prices.

As in these examples, nonlinear relations are the essence of the real world. Against this backdrop, the linear methods of classical statistics tend to be accurate only in limited niches dealing with proportional phenomena.

On the other hand, discontinuous linkages are the forte of machine learning. For this reason, knowledge systems permit a decision maker to analyze more complex problems than is feasible with statistics alone.

We return now to the analysis of customer profiling on the Web. For the task at hand, the predictive performance of neural networking, case based reasoning, and multiple regression were evaluated.

The data set was obtained from a public resource based on an online survey involving more than 5,000 Web users.[25] Questions had been posed on various topics such as user demographics, online privacy, security, and purchasing on the Net. For the knowledge mining application, the data file on demographics was merged with that on purchasing. A match of the files with unique ID values yielded a total of 900 cases. Among these, the first 700 cases were used as the training portion and the remainder as the test segment.

In predicting consumer behavior, it is often unclear which features should be employed as the explanatory variables. One way to approach this task lies in the selection of variables through statistical methods.

The statistical scheme known as stepwise regression was used to examine the complete collection of 76 variables or attributes of the respondents.[26] Among these, only seven variables had predictive value for the model:

- Household income
- Web access from home
- Skill level
- Use of online chat
- Experience in creating Web pages
- Hearing disability
- Age

It is curious to note the inclusion of hearing disability among the significant features. In retrospect, however, it seems plausible that a physical handicap might lead to a differential preference for shopping in realspace versus cyberspace.

To examine the utility of modern techniques, the statistical model was compared against a couple of adaptive procedures. The machine learning approaches consisted of case based reasoning and neural network models. For the CBR model, each prediction relied on the automatic selection of five precedent examples in the data base. Meanwhile, the neural network employed a learning procedure known as the backpropagation algorithm. After calibrating each adaptive scheme against the training data, it was tested on the remaining cases.

For the statistical model, the value of the average error in predicting the purchase index was 1.632. The corresponding values for the neural network and case base reasoning models were 1.425 and 1.391

respectively.[27] In other words, the CBR method bested the neural network, which in turn outperformed the statistical technique.

This application illustrates the utility of autolearning tools for online marketing. The years ahead will witness the continued ascent of knowledge mining across all domains, ranging from commerce and medicine to science and governance.

Hybrid of the Real and Unreal

"In the future, there will be no Internet companies." This byword emerged as the conventional wisdom at the turn of the century. More precisely, every enterprise would become a creature of the Net: the only differences would lie in the nature and extent of cyberization.

The fusion of the real and virtual realms can occur through a merger or diversification. An example of the former is found in the marriage of America Online, a provider of online services, with Time Warner, a traditional media firm with businesses ranging from magazines to movies.

An organization in rockspace can also diversify into bitville on its own. Unfortunately, venerable firms from the industrial era often adapted poorly to the frenzied pace of innovation in cyberspace. In the first wave of attempts, most projects to cyberize a brick enterprise met with failure.

A case in point was Wal-Mart, with its vision of selling everything to everyone on the planet. In 1996, the merchandiser began a partial exodus into bitville with some reservations and enthusiasm to match. Over the next three years, the firm launched a tepid foray into the Net, and was able to gain only a tenuous foothold.

Even as Wal-Mart floundered in strange terrain, it could not ignore the swift progress of competitors based in the virtual hinterland. From mid-1999, the retailer initiated a major campaign to capture a swathe of cyberia. For instance, the number of books offered at its online store stood at 50,000 at century's end, but was slated to burgeon to 700,000 within a few years.

A central feature of Wal-Mart's marketing campaign lay in convenience for customers. In particular, buyers could order products on the Web but return them, if they chose, on a visit to a physical store.

In the 1990s, online shopping was largely the province of upper-income consumers. As the Net began to penetrate further into the mainstream, however, it came to embrace lower-income surfers. Since these users represented War-Mart's main customer base, prospects for the merchandiser improved with the passage of time.

Despite the apparent potential of the Net, the retailer had a rough time on the digital trail. By 2001, online sales were still a miniscule fraction of its revenues. According to one survey, 100% of customers using the Website at Walmart.com experienced problems with their orders, ranging from shipping costs to wayward goods which never arrived. By comparison, 55% of customers at Amazon.com cited problems; in spite of the appalling figure, the level of dissatisfaction was still the lowest achieved by any online retailer.[28]

As Wal-Mart found to its dismay, entrenched players are no easier to displace in bitspace than in dirtspace. Since the dawn of commerce on the Web, Amazon has been the brand to beat in online retailing. And the pioneer was not pausing long enough for parvenus on the Net to catch up.

To cite an example of its virtuosity, Amazon expanded into the kiddie market by linking up with the physical retailer Toys 'R' Us. The toy chain had previously dabbled in virtual marketing but had given up in favor of a partnership with a veteran of the realm. According to the terms of the partnership, Toys 'R' Us was to provide the goods. Meanwhile, Amazon would run the toyseller's Website and ship product from its own network of omnibus warehouses. The alliance has been held up by industry observers as a success story in bridging the digital divide of atoms and bits.

The future will bring additional examples of synergism between the real and the unreal. Some of the marriages will be highly visible, as in the toy affair, while others will take place without ceremony. In the latter case, an enterprise on one side of the digital border will expand into the other under the guidance of hired guns from the opposing camp.

Lessons for Online Marketing

The realm of digital business is still in its infancy. Even so, the field has begun to show some recurrent patterns of behavior.

As a wild and woolly creature, the Net educes a measure of caution in novice users. Given the misgivings against any unfamiliar contraption, a newcomer has a natural tendency to be wary of both the network and its denizens.

For this reason, surfers tend to gravitate toward familiar names. In fact, respected retailers in realspace can charge online prices at a premium of 8 to 9% over "pure play" vendors which exist only in cyberland.[29]

The vital role of trust in securing customer loyalty highlights the importance of establishing brand identity backed by a sterling image of the overall enterprise. Although Netizens can change sites at the click of a mouse, they do not switch vendors with aimless abandon.

The importance of trust underscores the value of obtaining referrals to a virtual store from respected partners located both online and offline. The fact that most customers do not change allegiances lightly points to the value of "imprinting": winning a customer's business at the first opportunity.[30]

A newborn venture in cyberspace has to establish a name and a following. One way to accelerate the process is to forge alliances with reputable players.[31] For instance, a fledgling provider of software can offer its products via resellers such as renowned boutiques and discounters, or through referrals from portals and online publications.

Creating a partnership with a leading enterprise bestows credibility by association. It also raises visibility and expands the reach of both parties to new markets.

As in realspace, virtual customers value convenience and service. These traits should inform the entire marketing cycle, from the conception of a product to the point of sale and beyond. A winsome policy is to solicit feedback from the user and offer end-to-end service, including after-sale interaction.

Finally, informed customers tend to spend more. For this reason, an aggressive marketer would do well to provide timely, accurate information tailored to each user's needs. The customized functions can be supported by multimedia interfaces in concert with smart software to serve as personal guides to visitors.

Summary

The economic landscape around the planet is undergoing a radical transformation as a result of technical change, expanding trade, and capital mobility. In the first wave of virtualization, the volume of online commerce more than doubled each year.

For a hosting firm, a Website is both cost-effective and easy to maintain. On the Net, multimedia offers an attractive platform for marketing. As a case in point, the use of dynamic content such as video and animation allows for dashing displays and rapid comprehension by customers as well as partners.

A supply chain involves the entire cascade of functions starting with the acceptance of an order and ending with the delivery of the product. To remain competitive in a rapidly shifting environment, business processes have to be taken apart and rebuilt on a regular basis.

At the frontier of digital commerce, autolearning software can generate both descriptive and prescriptive knowledge for action. The goal of knowledge discovery is to extract useful insights from raw data.

For a vendor, smart software based on data mining is a versatile tool for one-to-one marketing. To illustrate, the marketing message can be tailored to a visitor in real time depending on the pattern of navigation through a Website.

This chapter has presented an application of knowledge systems in the task of predicting consumer behavior. In a competitive bout, cased based reasoning outperformed the neural network, which in turn bested multiple regression. The results illustrate the tendency of learning systems to prevail over the traditional methods of statistics.

The years ahead will witness the infusion of knowledge mining in all areas of management, ranging from trend assessment and market profiling to order processing and customer service. Knowledge discovery is a limber platform for differentiating products from a jumble of comparable offerings in the global arena. With such equipment in the armory, a resourceful strategist can drive deeply into far-flung markets and rescue impressionable customers from the clutches of rapacious rivals.

The judicious deployment of virtual technologies is imperative for survival in the 21st century. A firm which competes without a full complement of digital arms is likely to skip virtuality and proceed directly to oblivion.

Chapter 5

Competing with Bits

Cyberspace is the frontier of information technology as well as mainline commerce. Life in a strange land is fraught with hazards, and the realm of bits is no exception.

The ecology of the Web is governed by a severe set of rules. In the land of the digital, the quick fells the mighty. The advantage of speed covers the gamut of competitive factors, from technical prowess and product design to brand identity and market share.

The law of the cyberjungle leaves little room for complacency or hesitation. The pace of activity on the Net highlights the need for a coherent approach to molding a competitive strategy.

In the realm of the corporeal, a popular tool for the strategist is a framework for analyzing an industry through an array of competitive forces.[32] This scheme has been used extensively to analyze the entire spectrum of industries in the traditional economy. The strategic model has also been invoked in the past to assess basic applications of information technology.[33]

The strategic framework, along with a complementary set of models, may be extended to the Internet environment. For concreteness, the concepts are examined here in the context of the health care industry.

In addition, a comparative analysis explores the similarities and differences among vendors of goods and services in the digital sphere.

Background

The health care sector encompasses a wide variety of players. Among these are vendors of medical instruments and supplies; health maintenance organizations (HMO's) and other health plan providers; hospitals and nursing homes; home health care providers; medical laboratories; clinic management companies; and medical product distributors. These actors share common concerns as well as distinct traits.

In the literature on health care, however, the standard enterprise for competitive analysis is a hospital. For this type of business, the five forces driving an industry are as follows.

- *Competitors.* Established rivals in the industry include for-profit hospitals, not-for-profit clinics, religious hospitals, government hospitals, and community clinics.
- *Newcomers.* Relative newcomers to the industry range from HMO's to physician group practices and e-commerce providers.
- *Substitutes.* Alternatives to conventional health care options include wellness centers, health spas, holistic practitioners, and improved lifestyles.
- *Suppliers.* In the logistic chain for delivering services, upstream players range from real estate developers and construction firms to hospital suppliers, medical equipment vendors, and informatic providers.
- *Buyers.* Purchasers of medical services encompass both individuals and organizations: patients, physicians, employers, insurance companies, government agencies, and other hospitals.

The rapid growth of the Internet has led to the proliferation of products and services in every industry. The hectic expansion has been accompanied by a steady decline in the cost of switching vendors. Moreover, entry barriers have fallen due to low capital requirements, difficulty of differentiating products, and ready access to distribution.

All around the globe, vendors face fierce competition in the scramble for customers armed with extensive information about suppliers and their input factors. Moreover, technical progress occasionally scotches the need for a particular input or offers a better substitute.

Despite the wrenching transition — and also because of it — an enterprise has to set in place a systematic scheme for tracking technologies, monitoring rivals, and boosting agility. Further, a solid reputation and brand identity have become increasingly important in a turbid market churning with products and firms which pop up one day and vanish the next.

The promise of online commerce for enhancing productivity and economic growth can only be fulfilled by a coherent approach to planning and execution. The strategic model for digital advantage may be tailored to organizations in both newborn and mature industries. In this context, vanguard enterprises encompass independent start-ups as well as entrepreneurial groups within mature firms.

As indicated earlier, the competitive model represents a generic tool for scrutinizing an industry. For the sake of clarity, however, the concepts are explored in the context of online firms in the health care sector.[34] We examine the five factors as they pertain to two companies focusing on different segments of the industry. One contender is a merchandiser of pharmaceutical products, and the other a digital portal for health care services.

Competitive Analysis for a Dynamic Industry

The competitive environments for realspace and e-space exhibit a number of common attributes as well as divergent features. Despite the differences between the two realms, a uniform set of frameworks can be used to analyze both types of domains.

Environmental assessment. The environmental factors for a turbulent industry span the spectrum from technical advances and consumer tastes to economic trends and political winds. To be more precise, environmental issues include the following dimensions.

- Technical progress
- Strategic uncertainty
- High initial cost but steep cost reduction
- Embryonic rivals and spin-offs
- Pacesetting buyers
- Global economic trends
- Short planning horizon
- Subsidies from governmental or industrial sources

In rockspace, a firm faces mounds of risk from emerging technologies and the resulting uncertainty in the direction of nascent markets. However, an even greater hazard stems from the specific standards and product types which will come to dominate the market.

As a case in point, the Betamax and VHS formats represented competing standards in the nascent market for consumer video during the 1980s. For this market segment, the evolution of the respective technologies could be foreseen with relative ease. However, despite the superior technical features of the Betamax format, the VHS standard came to capture the consumer market. The victory of the inferior format was due largely to a winning combination of global alliances and promotional tactics among the proponents.

Digital technologies are advancing swiftly on all fronts. The rapid pace of developments in software, hardware, and systems implies a greater measure of technical uncertainty than that in the physical realm.

For a restless industry, a second category of risk lies in tactical uncertainty at the level of individual players. In the virtual sphere as in physical space, the optimal strategy for each player is difficult to divine. This is due in large part to the scarcity of hard data concerning competitors, customers and industry structure.

Operating facilities in high-tech industries are often characterized by daunting levels of investment. At the outset, lack of experience in conjunction with small batches combine to entail high costs per unit of production.

On the other hand, vanguard firms encounter a favorable learning curve. The steep decline in the average cost of production bestows great advantage on the market leader.

The contrasting duo of a large investment followed by plunging cost per unit is often accentuated in the virtual arena. For instance, a complex program may be expensive to develop but can be replicated at nearly zero marginal cost. The profile of the cost curve obviously depends on the technologies deployed in the business as well as the nature of a particular product line.

A dynamic industry bubbles with upstart ventures as well as spin-offs from going concerns. Employees often enjoy equity participation and expanding responsibilities due to rapid growth. In addition, the continual metamorphosis of both technologies and strategies results in a steady rate of innovations.

For the physical as well as virtual realms, the survival of a fledgling venture depends on speed and efficiency. After the infant stage, however, the myriad firms in the industry coalesce through restructuring, whether in the form of mergers, acquisitions or bankruptcies.

Against the shifting backdrop, the market pioneers encounter as well the reluctance of first time buyers. Consumers desire the benefits of the new technology but often hesitate to serve as guinea pigs for an unstable technology. On the other hand, a group of early adopters delights in novelty and the status of owning snazzy gadgets. The pacesetters are to be found in both the material and virtual realms.

Product information is readily available in e-space, including the structure of prices and terms of sale. Despite the wealth of online data, potential buyers may be reluctant to make a purchase unless they can "heft" the product in their hands. This is a hurdle which applies even more acutely to virtual vendors.

Infant industries are usually characterized by nimble players in a feverish contest to become the market leader. The haste in conjunction with the lack of experience in the field can result in poor planning and missed opportunities.

In the commercialization of a novel technology, the difficulties are compounded by sparse knowledge of viable revenue models. In the first wave of applications, entrepreneurs and financial markets often bestow lavish funds on new schemes regardless of profits or even revenues. The hype and hysteria for online schemes reached a climax on the eve of the millennium. Fortunately, the speculative bubble for Internet ventures burst in spring 2000 without crippling the global economy.

Emerging industries are supported at times through subsidies from the government. While these accommodations are welcomed by new firms, the inducements are vulnerable to the political climate. From a macrolevel perspective, the subsidies are likely to stunt the growth of an industry by shielding their beneficiaries from global competition. The coddling is detrimental to consumers and may well jeopardize the long-term viability of the protected industry. Over the long run, open markets are the nurseries of world-class firms.

Industry structure. The structure of an industry may be partitioned into a handful of factors or categories. The five factors take the form of rivalry, entry barriers, substitution threats, suppliers, and buyers.

The major determinants of *rivalry* in cyberspace are the following.

- Overall industry growth
- Fixed costs and sporadic overcapacity
- Product differences
- Brand awareness
- Information sources and switching costs for buyers
- Diversity and relative strengths of competitors
- Corporate investments and expected payoffs
- Barriers to entry and exit

The online sector is expanding at a breathtaking pace in line with a surge in product differentiation, and a slide in switching costs. In this competitive milieu, the path to success lies in design innovation, product quality and convenient delivery.

The second factor in industry structure is found in the collection of *entry barriers*. These competitive hurdles can take the following forms.

- Proprietary product differences
- Capital requirements and economies of scale
- Access to necessary inputs
- Structures for distribution
- Absolute cost advantages and learning curve
- Brand awareness
- Switching costs
- Expected retaliation
- Government policy

In virtual space, the barriers to entry have been falling as a result of declining capital requirements, difficulty in differentiating products, and easy access to distribution.

Another competitive factor is found in the threat of product *substitution*. This occurs, for instance, when cough drops are used in lieu of a liquid remedy. The salient characteristics of substitution are the following.

- Relative price and performance of substitutes
- Switching costs
- Buyer propensity to substitute

In the electronic world, alternative modes of communication represent potential threats to operating procedures and marketing channels. Examples lie in the use of video versus text or audio to convey similar information. The potential for substitution also applies to alternate technologies, as illustrated by satellite links versus grounded fibers for transmission, or the use of brokerage services versus personal software agents to seek information.

The next industry factor lies in *supplier power*. The core elements of this component are the following.

- Differentiation of inputs
- Switching costs of suppliers and producers in the industry
- Availability and cost of substitute inputs
- Scale economies and market concentration of suppliers
- Threat of forward integration by suppliers versus backward integration by producers in the industry

The supplier of an input factor faces threats which overlap those of vendors in general. In the digital realm, suppliers are subject to global competition. Meanwhile, buyers can easily obtain voluminous data about suppliers and their inputs. Moreover, technical innovation sometimes eliminates the need for an input or leads to attractive alternatives.

The last competitive factor takes the form of *buyer power*. The key attributes of this dimension include the following.

- Information available to purchasers
- Product differences
- Brand identity
- Price sensitivity
- Substitute products
- Switching costs
- Ability to integrate backward
- Concentration of buyers
- Incentives for decision makers

In the list above, the threat of backward integration springs from institutional rather than retail customers. For instance, a vendor of cellphones might decide to manufacture the components rather than merely assemble them. However, a consumer is less likely to behave in a similar fashion by constructing his own phone from modules procured separately.

Since buyers can easily obtain information on products on the market, they assume a dominant role in a commercial transaction. This is in contrast to an earlier age when vendors determined the product mix, leaving consumers with little say in the nature and features of individual offerings. To buy or not to buy: that was the only real question for a consumer in the age of mass production.

The preceding factors of competition apply to any industry, whether online or offline. To clarify the issues involved, we focus on two representative firms in the health care sector.

Industry Factors for a Merchandiser

Around the turn of the century, a horde of ventures rushed into the digital arena to carve out a niche in the health care sector. For the most part, the newbies dashing into cyberia ran off a cliff into the void of nonexistent markets, balking customers, and shifty technologies.

Another peril was the threat of entrenched giants based in realspace. The goliaths were slow and clueless, but their deep pockets allowed them to make any number of mistakes over the short term. In due course, the veterans of the rock world could also poach seasoned talent from vapory ventures which would burn up and blow away within a year or two.

The task of this section is to spotlight the central issues in crafting a virtual strategy. To avoid needless distraction, we will focus on a couple of generic enterprises rather than specific ventures in the health care sector.

The approach involves a comparative analysis of a merchandising outfit and a service provider. The merchandiser is a representative firm which we will christen Carebox.com.

On the other hand, the online service is a portal for medical information and communal interaction. In addition to serving consumers as a gateway to health care resources, the site offers administrative and ecommerce services among private physicians, community hospitals, and other suppliers. The portal, which we will call Haleport.com, is a composite of several real ventures which led the way during the first wave of migration to digitopia.

We begin here with the strategic milieu for Carebox.com. This retailer deals in drugs as well as personal care products such as cosmetics and nutritional supplements.

To generate a competitive profile for this player, we turn to the general framework for industry analysis. In the context of rivalry, the major determinants for the company are as follows.

- Brand recognition, selection, convenience, price, Website utility, customer service, reliability, and speed of order shipment
- Vulnerability of systems and operations to unforeseen problems
- Growth of the pharmaceutical market and Internet usage in general
- Marketing relationships with leading manufacturers and advertisers
- Distribution channels
- Competitors' alliances and strategies
- Financial resources
- Technical ability
- Tax benefits of online retailing
- Government regulation of the Internet

The entry barriers for Carebox range from government regulation to consumer loyalty. More pricisely, the key hurdles to entry take the following forms.

- *Customers.* Buyers must be attracted and retained affordably.
- *Physical distribution.* The drawbacks of traditional modes of distribution include inconvenience, narrow selection, sparse information, and lack of privacy.
- *Government regulations.* The fiats include constraints on pharmacies and the sale of over-the-counter drugs. Other standards relate to the confidentiality of patient records, or restrictions by the Food and Drug Administration (FDA) on drug advertising and promotion.
- *Strategic relationships.* Potential partners range from portals such as Yahoo to distributors such as Amazon.com. Others are corporeal retailers with the advantage of physical branches,

such as Rite Aid Corporation. Still others involve health care organizations, especially those in reimbursement or managed care.

The threat of substitute products for Carebox springs from alternative offerings by actual or potential competitors. However, the wholesale replacement of medication by alternative means is unlikely over the next few decades. Conventional drugs will prevail until the risk of ailments can be eliminated entirely through nanotechnology and biomedicine; but this development is improbable within the first quarter of the 21st century.

In the digital environment, Carebox faces a moderate amount of supplier power. Moreover, the company has to rely on partners for part of the order fulfillment process. The firm is also vulnerable to external forces on pharmaceutical costs and pricing policies.

An internal aspect of supplier power for the firm stems from its own personnel. The fate of the company is linked intimately to the skills of senior management as well as the ability to retain experienced personnel at all levels of the organization.

In the context of buyer power, the company faces a large array of players. The firm depends on reimbursement plans from third-party payors such as federal health agencies, private health insurers, health maintenance organizations, and other groups. Each category of players exerts some measure of buying power on the firm.

To position a company for strategic advantage, the enterprise has to define its mission, opportunities, strengths, weaknesses and threats. These factors represent distinct dimensions, yet they are highly interdependent. For instance, it is meaningless to define the mission of a firm without considering its organizational capabilities as well as external opportunities and potential threats.

We now turn to the task of environmental assessment for a provider of pure services. The discussion is attended by the targeting and resolution of critical issues in molding a virtual strategy.

Industry Factors for a Service

As a provider of informatic services in the health care sector, Haleport faces the same general environment as Carebox. As a result, many of its concerns are similar. In terms of rivalry, the central determinants of success for the portal are as follows.

- Compelling products, differentiated from those of competitors
- Proprietary technology
- Growth of Internet commerce and functionality
- Deployment of novel techniques and standards
- Customer base in the health care industry
- Financial, technical, marketing and other skills

A variety of entry barriers provide a measure of protection for Haleport. The hurdles for party crashers are as follows.

- Corporate technology, ranging from application software to security platforms
- Reputation and customer loyalty
- Strategic relationships with partners
- Procedures for managing a virtual organization
- Government regulation of the Internet, ranging from privacy and pricing to content, copyright, distribution, and product quality.

Haleport faces a perennial threat of substitution due to advances in software technologies. For instance, the years ahead will bring forth smarter software for compiling information and conducting transactions as agents for Netizens. This will reduce the need for information services from intermediaries such as Haleport.

The company is vulnerable to supplier power from both horizontal and vertical axes. In the latter direction, vendors of outsourcing services can choose to expand downstream. Moreover, large providers – such as HMO chains or insurance firms – may decide to expand horizontally.

For a firm such as Haleport, customers often wield a big stick due to their aggregation into clubs of one sort or another. Examples of large customers are clinical laboratories, HMO's, preferred provider organizations, and medical groups such as clinical associations.

The competitive profile of a firm can be mapped by depicting its mission (M) in the midst of opportunities (O) and threats (T) in the environment, while taking into account the organization's internal strengths (S) and weaknesses (W). A MOSWT diagram for Haleport is shown in Figure 5.1.

A firm has to maneuver in a landscape trafficked by allies, rivals, and other stakeholders. Figure 5.2 depicts the field of forces and their constituent elements. Haleport has to develop a suitable relationship with each of the key players in its sphere. Some of the players are to be competitors and others partners. Still others embody both roles: the parties involved might compete in one market while collaborating on basic research, product standards, and other issues of common concern.

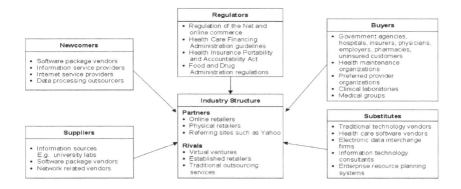

Fiure 5.1. A MOSWT diagram for Haleport.

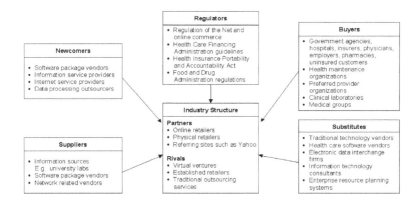

Figure 5.2. Field of forces for Haleport.

For a practical scenario, each component of the strategic model should be elaborated into finer levels of detail. As a case in point, the competitive threats for a firm include risks in the marketplace; the latter in turn might encompass government regulations, strategic partnerships, and consumer tastes. The network of relationships among the varied elements constitutes a causal map of linked nodes. For illustration, a causal chart of competitive threats for Haleport is depicted in Figure 5.3.

The construction of a competitive strategy must take into account an assortment of issues ranging from technical expertise to customer needs. A winsome strategy has to be backed up by policies which govern the routine operation of an organization from day to day. A causal map of the prime factors behind an operating policy for Haleport is presented in Figure 5.4.

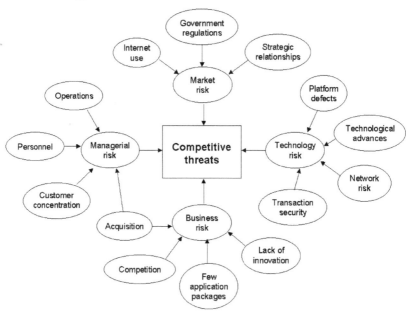

Figure 5.3. Causal map of competitive threats for Haleport.

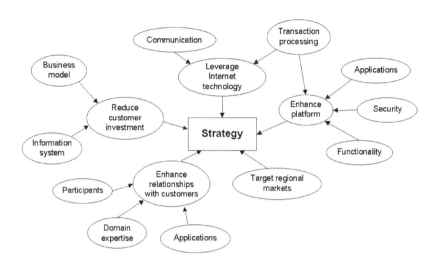

Figure 5.4. Causal map of strategy and policy for Haleport.

In cyberspace, the competitive strategies for merchants and service providers exhibit common features as well as distinct traits. The next section presents a comparative profile of these two types of vendors.

Merchandise vs. Service Vendors

A great variety of firms have set up shop in cyberia. Among the multitude of online ventures, we can discern a number of commonalities as well as differences among the players. We begin by examining the generic features among providers of goods and services.

Similarities. The common attributes of competitive strategy for merchandise and service providers range from customer characteristics to operating policies.

● *Availability.* A vendor's Website can be accessed 24 hours a day throughout the year.

- *Convenience.* Customers can obtain information and shop anywhere, whether at home, in an office or in transit.
- *Personalization.* An Internet platform may be shared among collaborating firms, but tailored to fit the needs of particular clients. An example of a customized feature is a smart agent which responds to a question on nutrition after considering personal characteristics such as the user's age and weight.
- *Reputation.* A sterling image of the products and services at a Website promotes visits and purchases.
- *Safety.* Confidentiality of records and security in the network are prime considerations for customers.
- *Scale of Virtual Network.* Marketing partners can refer customers, while virtual communities such as chat rooms tend to enhance loyalty.
- *Quality.* Performance and dependability are crucial features for products, along with the dependability of delivery and maintenance.

The front office, whether made of bricks or bits, is the lobby where the public meets the enterprise. This forum is a prime candidate for distinguishing the firm from its competitors.

The services on offer to the visitor have to blend the goals of friendliness and responsiveness with courtesy and efficiency. The task of the front office is to provide services tailored to each guest in spite of the diversity of requirements and tastes among customers.

The function of the back office, on the other hand, is to support the activities of the front office. Although the interior venue is shielded from public view, its efficacy has a palpable impact on the image of the organization. The public forum cannot offer a satisfactory experience for the customer if the back room is unresponsive. When the logistics arm fails to process orders accurately or to resolve bottlenecks promptly, the customer will turn to a rival that will.

Many of the goals and tactics for an enterprise in bitland are no different from those in dustville. For this reason, the strategies for merchandise vendors often resemble those of service providers.

Differences. Since a merchandiser deals in physical goods while a service vendor does not, a strategy or policy for one cannot fully cover the other. The differential concerns for merchandise and service firms span a rainbow of issues from customer needs to internal procedures.

A key axis of divergence is found in *pricing*. For a merchandiser such as Carebox, online customers are usually sensitive to price. As a result, surfers tend to travel online among a variety of vendors in search of low prices.

On the other hand, competing on price is not as effective in services as it is with products. Since service offerings are difficult to compare beforehand, consumers rely more on reputation and prior experience for their purchasing decisions.

In shopping for goods, convenience in browsing and ordering is a basic functional requirement. Moreover, the mechanism for returning unwanted merchandise can be decisive: customers desire a fall-back option if they find a product to be unsuited to their needs of the moment.

For a consumer of services, convenience in ordering and delivery is also important. However, the importance of convenience depends largely on the type of product under consideration. For instance, ease of access may be instrumental in ordering a song in MP3 format, but less vital for a professional program to handle corporate finance.

As for timeliness, the speed of transactions in the front office is vital for all vendors. An example in this category lies in responsiveness to customer queries. For merchandisers, the swift delivery of goods through physical space is critical.

On the other hand, timeliness for a service provider will depend on the type of transaction. For this sector, promptness in the back office is a key determinant of success: the speed of information exchange, transaction processing, and work flows.

Novelty is a vital feature for merchandisers, as customers desire the latest and best products at a given level of price. In contrast, a service outfit has to focus on usability as much as novelty. The provider must deploy standardized technologies, user interfaces, and delivery platforms among the target group of customers. The latest data and features can be a selling point, but novelty of the service offering is not the overriding attraction. For instance, many Netizens continue to employ an old version of a Web browser even when the latest and greatest is available for free.

Marketing strategies must necessarily differ between providers of goods and services. For instance, an online vendor of a physical product has limited ability to entice customers with product samples.

By contrast, a provider of services can often issue free samples. Examples in this category lie in old issues of magazines, limited subscription periods, 30-day demo software, and so on.

The nature and importance of distribution networks differ for vendors of hard and soft goods. When dealing with physical products, effective logistics are vital for manufacturers, wholesalers, and retailers.

For many services in the world of bricks, distribution is a secondary factor. As example is a diner or a hairdresser. The same is true in the virtual realm for a different reason: namely, immediate access to the Web for online customers.

Vendors of real and virtual products face differential network effects. For merchants of goods, the network externalities tend to be indirect. To illustrate, the preponderance of machines compatible with the IBM PC, in concert with its open standards, has resulted in a larger market than that for Macintosh computers. The upshot has been keener competition, swifter innovation, lower costs, and wider range of products for the PC federation. The attendant size of the market has been a gold mine for the vendors of both hardware and software.

For service vendors, on the other hand, network externalities tend to be more direct. To illustrate, a software agent which can negotiate appointments for its owner is more useful if everybody else has similar software. The proliferation of such digital tools increases productivity for customers as well as brand awareness for the vendor.

The preceding set of competitive issues provides a logical framework for evaluating an industry, positioning a firm, and developing a competitive strategy. The discussion has focused on virtual ventures in the health care sector.

Even so, the tools of competitive analysis are generic. They apply to any firm, whether in a mature or infant industry, and regardless of its location in realspace or nonspace. Whatever its origins, each firm has to take account of strategic factors in both the physical and virtual realms.

In the final analysis, the only viable strategy for the long term is the creation of economic value: the difference between high revenues from delighted customers and low costs through efficiency in procurement and operations.[35] Here is one guiding principle from the past which will continue to ring true in the millennium.

Summary

The Net is a boundless arena for commerce and economic growth. In cyberspace, a slew of factors resemble those of traditional commerce, while a heap of others are distinct.

A renowned framework for competitive strategy takes account of the competitive forces in a given industry. Over the years, this model has served as a basis for positioning companies in diverse industries.

This chapter has shown how the analytical framework can be extended to the Internet environment. For concreteness, the concepts were examined in the context of the health care industry. In addition, a comparative analysis delved into the similarities and differences for firms which proffer goods or services in cyberia.

The rapid growth of online commerce highlights the need for a systematic approach to competitive analysis and strategy formulation. Many concepts from realspace may be ported to e-space, as exemplified by the following characteristics.

- Branding is a key to competitive advantage.
- The focus of competition shifts from technology to customer needs as an industry matures.
- Strategic partners are vital for swift dominance in technology, distribution, and brand awareness.
- Industry players consolidate under the press of scale economies in operations, marketing, and product innovation.

On the other hand, a variety of factors differentiate competition in bitspace as opposed to rockspace. The salient concepts include the following.

- Pace of innovation is faster, powered by new software and hardware advances.
- Global reach is immediate.
- Start-up costs can be insignificant.
- Marginal cost of incremental business is usually trivial.

Within the realm of electronic commerce, a number of characteristics distinguish the marketing of goods versus services. The divergent aspects include the following.

- Price competition is more severe for the merchandise segment.
- Novelty and value are vital for merchandise customers.
- Ability to provide trial samples is limited for physical goods.
- Network externalities are often indirect.

The guidelines above provide a starting point for developing a competitive strategy. However, the steady pace of innovation in cyberspace will continue to reshape the principles of competition. The only certitude is that the millennium will bring even more turmoil, with dangers for the slow and rewards for the quick.

Chapter 6

Vanguards of the Millennium

Charged with the energy of a frontier, cyberspace is progressing so swiftly that most predictions are likely to grow stale before their time. Amidst the turmoil, it would be foolhardy to attempt a sweeping preview of coming attractions.

On the other hand, a number of developments will ensue from innovations which have been demonstrated as prototypes or applications today. Our task here is to explore several avenues of growth in cyberville based largely on the techniques and trends presented in the preceding chapters.

The advent of speedy channels in wireless networks, coupled with smart software, promises a new generation of advanced services in digitopia. Until the turn of the century, online services had relied largely on supplying information on an "as is" basis. Examples of wares in this category are reports of traffic status or stock prices.

On the other hand, learning software offers a way to synthesize information into higher-level knowledge. Moreover, the results can be tailored to the general level of expertise of the user as well as the needs of the moment. For instance, a request for information on city hall might be covered by a leisurely presentation if issued from a living room, but more tersely if dispatched from a car in heavy traffic.

The years ahead will witness a cornucopia of knowledge based services on the Net. With increasing scope, the offerings will be mediated by personal agents which understand natural language and respond in kind.

An adept agent has to work in a distributed environment bristling with a mélange of hardware platforms, database structures, and application programs. To this end, a virtual aide has to function flexibly in a complex network and deal with specialized agents of all types.

This chapter covers the technologies behind nimble software, mobile media, and advanced services. In the interest of clarity, a general framework for implementing adaptive software is presented through case studies in product selection and environmental assessment. Finally, the chapter closes with some musings on the changing complexion of our digital society.

Bitland is Everywhere

The Internet offers a universal platform for the stockpile of information being digitized all over the globe. With the wireless Web, access is possible at any time and place within the scope of network services. Moreover, multimedia formats provide a dynamic channel for presenting information. For instance, the active role of the user in navigating a virtual world, coupled with the instant response of the system, yield an immersive experience which can linger in the mind long after the interaction has transpired.

The rapid growth of wirefree communication and the explosion of digitized knowledge highlight the need for mobile interaction based on intelligent agents. To illustrate this type of application, the overall configuration for a wireless system is depicted in Figure 6.1.

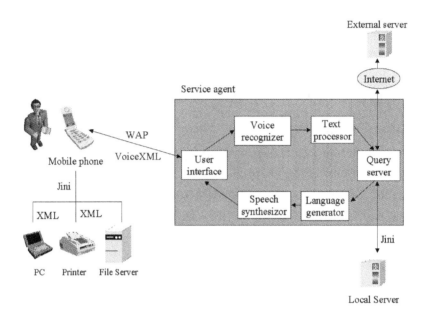

Figure 6.1. Overall architecture for a mobile Web-based service.

The system incorporates a variety of modules to provide advanced services on the mobile Net. The configuration employs software conventions such as the Wireless Application Protocol (WAP) for communicating with mobile devices; the eXtended Markup Language (XML) and its offspring for intelligent document processing; plus the Jini standard for automatic recognition and interaction among hardware units. A particular instance of XML is the Wireless Markup Language (WML), which is the mobile counterpart of the HyperText Markup Language employed on the Web for displaying documents on full-sized screens.

In the conventional Web environment, JavaScript is the standard language for encoding active behavior in a browser. The analogous scheme in the mobile context is the Wireless Markup Language Script

(WMLScript), a format for implementing simple types of adaptive behavior in a personal agent.

Amongst the surge of emerging technologies, one crest is found in autonomous learning. The maturation of machine learning over the past few decades has led to deft systems which can tailor a presentation not only to the basic level of expertise for a particular user, but to his or her changing level of knowledge. The adaptive features may be implemented through techniques such as case based reasoning, neural networks, or inductive resoning.

Digital intelligence can serve as the kernel of a genial aide for tailored presentations. With increasing frequency, agents which talk, sing and dance are popping up in applications ranging from information retrieval and product selection to personal negotiation and online entertainment.

Smart Shopping

The business environment has changed dramatically over the past century. The world has become a small and dynamic marketplace as never before.

To complicate matters, product lifecycles have become increasingly transient due to the progression of technical skills and customer expectations. These trends have driven vendors to (a) squeeze out costs throughout the production process, (b) diversify their product portfolios, (c) improve product quality, (d) focus on profitable customers, and (e) coordinate the sources of demand, supply and production across a global network.

The rapid diffusion of the Web is facilitating greater interaction – and potential opportunities for customization – between vendors and consumers. For instance, virtual reality and multimedia displays allow a buyer to envision a product design before actual fabrication.

A new paradigm, mass customization, emerged in the 1990s to supplant the traditional mode of mass production. Thanks to the ease of acquiring information and tailoring specs, a consumer can create her own design and request a product directly from the vendor.

The acceleration of business activity and the complexity of production processes underscore the need to deploy adroit systems in all stages of product design, operation, and distribution. A learning agent can automate routine tasks, convert data into knowledge, and make basic decisions for its owner. The software can be deployed as a plug-in module to serve as a personal aide on a desktop device, or deployed as a mobile agent on a global network for enterprise integration.

An exemplar of smart software to assist both consumers and producers is found in a program for product configuration. The goal of the system is to determine a suitable product design by adapting customer preferences and constraints using knowledge based methods. In addition, the agent employs virtual reality to provide a friendly interface to the user.

For clarity, the concepts are presented in the context of a digital aide for designing a personal computer. However, the central ideas are generic and therefore applicable to interactive systems in any domain.

Agents of Consumers and Producers

The soaring scope and pace of online transactions highlights the need for clever agents to assist in decision making. Ideally, a program should embody greater functionality than merely fetch files or issue raw data. Rather, an intelligent agent should be able to perform routine tasks autonomously, glean knowledge from disparate databases, and improve its own performance through experience.

As indicated in Chapter 2, the objective of data mining is to support decision making through the effective use of information. The field of knowledge mining covers adaptive procedures to discover patterns, trends, or relations in databases.

In complex domains, autolearning software can often find subtle patterns which elude human analysts. Moreover, automated tools can stand watch patiently over abstruse systems such as financial markets, adapting in real time to sudden disturbances.[36]

A prototype of a smart agent for decision making lies in an advisor for product selection. The system was designed for use in selecting a configuration for a personal computer.[37]

The aide employs the Virtual Reality Modeling Language to generate 3-dimensional views of selected designs. A graphic model can help a user envision a product as well as learn how to operate it.

In addition to helping the customer, the system can provide vendors with a tool for lowering cost and increasing productivity. More precisely, the efficiency of the design or assembly process can be improved by automatically retrieving precedent cases which bear on the task at hand.

While choosing a personal computer, a student might settle on a machine of modest means and a budget price to match. On the other hand, a professional might well require a computer with high performance even at a hefty price. Moreover, a prospective customer may wish to learn not only about the overall profile and price of the system but in addition the shape, functionality, or manufacturer for each component.

To date, numerous systems have been crafted to support decision making through artificial intelligence. In particular, expert systems were widely deployed in the 1980s to automate product design and process planning in various industries.

However, the rigidity of the rule-based approach in an expert system is inadequate for a rapidly changing environment. In a dynamic milieu, a program has to be flexible enough to accommodate novel requirements and constraints. Ultimately, a system should be able to furnish a new design automatically in line with a buyer's specs.

A customer is influenced by a wide range of factors, both topical and enduring. Since demographic information such as age and gender are key determinants of consumer behavior, an intelligent agent should strive to procure such information. Demographic data may be used in conjunction with product specs chosen by similar customers in the past.

During an online interaction, the target case is defined by the functional requirements of the customer as well as his personal profile. A collection of requirements and demographics constitutes the case base of "problems", while the attendant designs represent "solutions". The cases in the historical record may then be classified into distinct groups or clusters using a type of neural network known as a self-organizing map.[38]

In view of its flexibility, case based reasoning is also employed by the agent. First, CBR is closely related to human learning: people take account of observations and utilize them for future decision making. Second, the CBR methodology can be effective even if the knowledge base is sparse or peppered with imperfect data.

A design task is defined by three types of features: demographic factors, user requirements, and brand loyalty. The demographic category includes sex, age, income level, occupation, and educational level. The class of user requirements covers price, performance, design, and after-sale service. Because of its critical role, the third and final category consists of a single factor: brand loyalty.

During an interactive session, the current problem or target case specified by the user is first matched against the best selection of precedent cases. Next, the corresponding solutions are retrieved and modified to yield the desired result.

The agent then presents the candidate designs to the user. Information on the outcome is presented through HTML in one frame of the user's screen, while a 3-dimensional representation of the device is provided in a separate pane.

If the user would like to replace any of the components with another device, he can request a visual display of alternative modules which are compatible with the overall design. Examples in this category are found in external speakers or cameras. The user may also "open up" his virtual PC and inspect the components within.

In brief, the digital agent analyzes a set of user requirements and demographic features obtained through online interaction. The system recommends a computer design based on precedent cases, provides a graphic interface using virtual reality, and accommodates a customer's desire to explore alternative options.

To varying degrees, adroit aides of this type have begun to appear on a variety of Websites. Over the coming years, clever agents of sundry form will fill every niche of the virtual landscape.

Keeping Tabs on the World

Macrolevel trends and momentous events, by definition, have sweeping repercussions for individuals, companies, and governments. In this vein, examples of critical events include the Cuban Missile Crisis of the 1960s, the OPEC oil shock in the 70s, the Latin American debt crisis of the 80s, the Iraqi invasion of Kuwait at the turn of the 90s, and the terrorist attacks on the U.S. at the dawn of the millennium. Plainly, environmental monitoring and crisis forecasting are vital tasks for any pacesetter, whether in the private or public sector.

A smart system for environmental tracking, risk assessment, and event forecasting can draw on learning methods and visualization tools. In parallel with data mining and graphic modules, the system may incorporate natural language processing to convert text into semantic databases.

Knowledge mining schemes such as case based reasoning can identify similar patterns of events, while induction and other methods may forecast complex processes such as shifts in political risk. Moreover, interactive features such as virtual reality on Web-based platforms provide smooth interfaces for the rapid digestion of complex patterns.

Traditionally, environmental monitoring has been an intractable function assumed by senior executives and top-tier analysts of major organizations. Due to the complexity of the task, external assessment was largely a qualitative process which offered little or nothing in the way of formal tools.

Since the 1970s, however, the situation began to change with advances in decision science and information technology. One promising thrust emerged from the area of linguistic processing. In particular, software routines could automatically convert natural text into a sequence of semantic relationships, thereby paving the way for the automated interpretation of documents.

A sample task in this category is found in the encoding of a news article which examines relations between two countries. After breaking down each sentence into syntactic components, a document can be analyzed and transformed into a table of semantic linkages. Objects and relationships in the resulting database can then be interpreted in the context of the application domain.

To illustrate, a political analyst might wish to identify the patterns of sanguine or belligerent behavior among the players in a multilateral relationship. This type of software is exemplified by the Kansas Event Data System.[39] The encoding of events into a semantic database allows for ready analysis using a variety of statistical tools. For instance, clustering techniques can spotlight similar patterns of behavior, while statistical methods can pinpoint anomalies in a database.

Knowledge systems allow for even greater sophistication. In particular, schemes such as neural networks or case based reasoning can uncover intricate patterns or forecast chaotic processes. Data mining tools tend to be more effective at tasks of discrimination or forecasting than the use of statistical tools alone.[40]

The goals of an executive information system (EIS) include various functions in environmental assessment. A comprehensive EIS has to draw on data warehousing and knowledge mining schemes as well as multimedia tools to support monitoring activities.

In one executive system under development, the architecture incorporates dynamic features such as virtual reality on the Internet. Moreover, digital agents equipped with autolearning skills are designed to automate the monitoring function.

The overall configuration for the knowledge system is shown in Figure 6.2. The architecture comprises two main components: the basic module and the executive information system. The basic unit contains a natural language system which converts ordinary text or speech into a database of events. The language nodule relies on software which is available commercially.

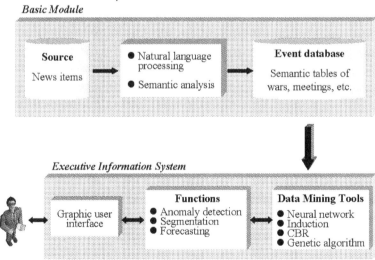

Figure 6.2. Architecture of an executive system for environmental monitoring, risk assessment, and crisis forecasting.

The second module is the core EIS, which draws on records in the event database. Learning techniques such as neural networks then convert the input into useful knowledge. Examples of target functions include the detection of aberrations or the identification of latent relationships among events. The results of the analysis are presented to the user through a friendly Web interface using tridimensional graphics.

This type of EIS is under development at a number of research centers.[41] In the years to come, adaptive systems for monitoring trends and anticipating shocks will transform high-level decision making in business, government, and think tanks around the world.

Denizens of Cyberia

The Internet and its attendant tools have given rise to new modes of communication. Surfers depend on the Web for both work and play, in tranquil solitude or frenzied interaction. Meanwhile, organizations both large and small rely on the Net for routine operations as well as crisis management. An intranet employs the technology of the Internet to support communication among the organization's employees, while extranets facilitate interaction with extramural partners and customers.

In all these activities, users rely increasingly on dynamic media and smart agents. A hallmark of the second wave of cyberization is a vivid agent, both personal and personable, to assist its owner throughout the course of the day.

According to one scenario in science fiction, virtual space is so compelling that some people will saunter in and lose the will to leave. The real world is a mere shadow of the sparkle in bitland, where the senses can enjoy whatever the mind can conceive.

The hypnotic power of cyberspace may appear far-fetched to sensible folks. Even so, reality has a way of encroaching upon fiction faster than anyone can imagine.

A small case in point lay in the Tamagotchi craze which broke out in Japan in the late 90s, then flared into a pandemic which seized schoolchildren around the planet. A smitten youngster would fixate on the care and feeding of a digital pet to the exclusion of incidental pursuits such as schoolwork.

One strain of virtual lures can force ruinous submission from its human host, often in the body of an impressionable teenager. A telltale sign of the affliction arises when the host takes up residence in an asphyxiating game parlor. The victim is driven day and night by the spellbinding software, and winds up ignoring worldly demands such as food and sleep.

Asia has turned into a mecca of digital parlordom, on occasion hosting international competitions for multiuser games. In an excess of zeal while training for a digital Olympiad, a number of wannabe stars pushed themselves over the edge, beyond cyberia and straight into nirvana. With increasing frequency, the evening news reported incidents of devotees collapsing from stress or even dropping dead of heart attacks.

In the otherworld of cyberland, a hapless person can readily lose his wealth as well as health. An example relates to the game of Lineage, a multiplayer world of knights and princesses. The game was developed for the Korean market in 1998, then exported to other countries the following year. The game exhibits the property of *persistence*, in which changes in a virtual world endure over time. For instance, the destruction of a building is permanent, as is the loss of a weapon.

So valuable are the soft weapons in Lineage that hot players would exchange them for cold cash in hard space. The value of digital assets rose inexorably as online warriors bid up their prices. By the summer of 2000, a number of virtual objects were each traded for "dirt world" cash of thousands of U.S. dollars. A conventional market in digital properties emerged, with online ads from entrepreneurial players offering virtual goods for sale.

The electronic economy attracted increasing numbers of outlaws and the inevitable escalation of criminal activity. Within a year, dozens of felons were booked by Korean police against extant legal statutes such as malicious hacking or commercial fraud.

On the other hand, a number crimes in cyberia had only nebulous links to realspace which could be used to invoke existing laws. In one incident reported on the evening news in late 1999, a player was driven to distraction by a serial thief who kept on stealing the former's weapons. The aggrieved party finally stomped into a police station and charged the miscreant with burglary. Unfortunately, the industrious agents of the law were uncertain of the legal grounds for prosecution: can a person be charged in rockland for a virtual crime restricted solely to bitland?

To bemused bystanders, the entire incident appeared ludicrous at first sight. On the other hand, it was worth noting that the crime might be virtual, but the loss of assets was real.

To an increasing extent, there is no clear demarcation between realspace and nonspace. As digitopia expands in both scope and depth, the border is becoming increasingly porous.

The Net harbors virtual neighborhoods where a settler can acquire a new identity and enjoy all manner of attractions, including the trappings of the real world. A digital citizen can play games, fall in love, raise a family, and buy a house. He can trade virtual goods or earn wages in cybercash for deposit in an electronic safe. He can also transfer digital funds from a virtual bank into an account at a concrete institution, then withdraw paper bills from a physical kiosk to purchase a real scooter. Work in virtuality and play in reality; or earn in dustville and spend in bitland; the worlds are there for choosing and mixing according to personal taste.

In our age of abstraction, numerous institutions have already migrated to cyberia to a greater extent than we generally acknowledge. During a conventional scam involving a wealthy victim in the real world, the loss of a sizeable chunk of assets might be perceptible only as the transfer of a decimal point on the target's bank balance. In the developed economies today, much of the wealth takes digital form.

At present, cyberia is still a gruff frontier with primal amenities and paltry rewards: a rambling concoction of pallid hues, tinny tones, and jerky flows. Despite the blemishes, though, some of us already find the call of virtuality irresistible.

By the middle of the 21st century, implanted chips in the brain will be able to provide direct connections from computerized worlds into sensory receptors in the nervous system. What will happen when the virtual is palpably richer than the physical? When the simulation becomes more intense than the reality, how much of our time will we choose to spend in realspace?

The rush of ornery questions presses beyond the individual and knocks on the future of civilization. Will the torrent of communications among the tribes of the world lead to a unity of spirit, or split the globe into a rubble of sects? How will we relate to smart agents when they have the capacity to learn without bound and to outgrow their human creators?

Will the promise of digitopia turn into a dystopia rather than a utopia? In the land of the virtual, the promise and the threat are inseparable . . . .

Welcome to the real world of the unreal.

Summary

The realm of the atom is expanding at a frenzied rate into the sphere of data. Despite some fanciful projections on the eve of the millennium, however, the move has so far been an extension rather than an abandonment of the physical world. The attractions of bitland have complemented rather than supplanted the structures and institutions of rockville.

The resources of the Internet can enhance the efficiency of both individuals and enterprises. Productivity increases with the automation of routine activity such as dispatching orders, authorizing payment, and preparing reports. Moreover, the effectiveness of ad hoc tasks can be bolstered by a fraternity of smart agents. Networked aides have at their disposal the wealth of online data as well as the means to distill knowledge from raw facts.

The riches of digitopia include products and services which were merely quixotic in an earlier age. These include the immersive experience of virtual worlds accessible at the touch of a button, as well as the ability to interact in a single event with millions of peers around the globe.

Today, virtual forums are hampered by constraints in bandwidth, availability, and content. In spite of the rough edges, however, many surfers already prefer to consort in cyberspace rather than dusty space. As the restrictions of digital interaction continue to dissolve, the lure of dataland will become even more compelling.

Folks in advanced economies have come to depend on the Net to contact friends around the clock and to acquire news on the run. As people everywhere join the ranks of Netizens, cyberspace will continue to expand as the universal forum for learning, leisure and labor.

Chapter 7

The Living Net

With the advent of the World Wide Web in the early 1990s, the Internet slipped into the mainstream of society. Since then, steady advances in speed and functionality have ensured a place for the Net in every niche of modern life.

During the years to come, any smart device—be it an appliance, monitor or rover—is likely to hook up with the Web. In the cauldron of innovation that is cyberspace, a cascade of transformations is certain to arise. One of these should lead to the emergence of self-awareness on the Net. The Web already harbors adept programs which learn from experience and evolve over time. At some point during the 21st century, the multitude of deft nodes should display adaptive behavior as a whole.

A variety of systems can already repair themselves to some degree. A primitive example from the early days of information theory is found in a self-correcting procedure: a program which detects and automatically mends mistakes in a message caused by extraneous signals in a telecommunication line. Today, certain devices linked to the Net can heal themselves by recovering from internal glitches or remolding their configuration after external shocks.

Residence in cyberville is not limited to mechanical objects. In increasing numbers, people and animals will also share the nexus. The Web will then become an evolving system of adaptive entities. The Internet, which began life as a network of networks, will turn in due course into a mind of minds.

The first part of this book has presented the foundations of the Internet. The survey included a brief history of the Net as well as a discussion of the core technologies. The birth of the Internet and its adoption by technologists of all stripes marked the first generation of the platform.

The subsequent chapters delved into a panoply of applications as well as strategies for harnessing the Web. The Net is a ubiquitous platform for improving productivity at the office or in the classroom, and for enhancing well-being within the home or out in the open. The diffusion of the Internet into mainline society represents the second generation of the infrastructure.

This final chapter, unlike the others, looks mainly toward the misty future. The developments on the horizon will emerge from current projects on the drawing boards and lab benches around the globe.

Some of the projections in this chapter seem well-nigh inevitable. Other scenarios, on the other hand, are more speculative. Musings of the latter type are prone to fumbling, much like groping across strange terrain in the dark. Yet history also teaches that flights of fancy often turn out to be too timid: the reality comes to surpass the imagination in both scope and depth.

Net Wit

The future will be an outgrowth of projects under way today. One line of development now taking shape is found in creative software.

An example of adept software comes, appropriately enough, from the field of biology. Through a process of evolution, a learning program has been able to reverse engineer the network of chemical reactions behind a physiological process. In one experiment, the objective of the software was to determine the metabolic pathways for a biochemical process known as the phospholipid cycle. Since the correct model was already known to biologists, it could serve as a test bed for the algorithm.

The input data for the program was the sequence of chemical concentrations for the compounds involved in the reactions. After grinding through multiple rounds of genetic evolution, the program automatically constructed an electrical network to serve as a structural model of the biochemical process. The final model exhibited the correct topology for the network of chemical reactions as well as the proper rate of activity for each step.[42]

As illustrated by this program, efforts are under way in research centers around the world to construct learning software which can improve their performance over time. Nimble programs have begun to fashion designs in diverse realms, ranging from music and artwork to medicine and architecture.

The maturation of evolutionary procedures will mark the third generation of the Internet. This stage will begin in the second decade of the millennium and last around four decades. In the age of synthetic evolution, virtual agents will support human activity across the board, and surpass manual performance in numerous fields.

The advantage of software agents over human principals is illustrated by a study in financial markets. The simulation involved a group of traders engaged in a continuous auction. In this setting, any player with adequate resources could propose a transaction at any time: offering goods for sale or presenting bids to buy an asset. The rules of the game were based on the standard protocols used in the real world for trading stocks, commodities, futures, and other instruments.

The participants in the simulated auction comprised both human players and software agents. Over the course of six experiments, the agents repeatedly edged out the humans. The winnings garnered by the robots exceeded those of humans by roughly 20% on average.

During the experiments, the performance of humans tended to improve over time as they became more comfortable with the simulation. Even so, the surplus earned by the robots surpassed that of humans by about 6% in the final rounds of each experiment.[43]

Once constructed and deployed, an agent works more swiftly and consistently than a person. Since virtual bots can trounce human players, electronic markets of the future are likely to become the exclusive domain of software. The competition between human principals will then turn into a contest of their agents as proxy champions.

Some highlights of the third era of the Internet are listed in Table 7.1. The first entry in the exhibit relates to creative agents. Inventive software will be the offspring of projects in automated creativity begun in the last quarter of the 20th century. Over the years, digital artists have produced drawings, melodies, and other compositions with flair. Some of the handiworks have been alluring enough to fetch cold cash from human buyers. Autonomous evolution, guided by feedback from a human audience, sets the stage for creativity without limit.

Table 7.1. Creative Net. The third generation of the Internet will span the period from about 2011 to 2050.

Feature	Sample Application
Creative software	Evolving programs which complement or surpass human designers
Genial agents	Autonomous programs which learn from each other without human intervention
Neural implants	Computer chips in the brain
Global minds	Instant communication among any group of persons and/or devices
Extrasolar Web	Interstellar craft as probes into deep space.

In the decades ahead, many people will find instant access to cyberspace to be an utter necessity. The executive will have to monitor market events as they transpire; the researcher will need to attend online conferences; a parent will want to keep track of his infants; and the soldier will have to monitor the battlefield. Members of the informatic society will hardly be able to make a decision without consulting some source or other on the Web.

For this reason, individuals will want to link more tightly to the nexus. In increasing numbers, people will also find it useful to interact with other entities—both human and artificial—in virtual worlds hosted on the network.

To ensure responsiveness, Netizens will not merely carry or even wear devices for linking to the network. Rather, many surfers will choose to obtain implants in order to stay in touch around the clock.

For good measure, the biochips for communication will be accompanied by accessories to supplement human memory as well as nanoscale robots to help regulate bodily functions. These devices will not require an artificial source of energy, as they should run on the same biochemical reactions which power a human organ.

Out of this World

As we saw in Chapter 2, the Internet that is near and dear to us employs a handful of versatile standards. The main conventions are the Transmission Control Protocol (TCP) and the Internet Protocol (IP).

The duo of standards, known to its friends as TCP/IP, conveys a lengthy message as a collection of small packets. When a client device requests a document from a server, the interaction takes the form of a running dialogue. To illustrate, the request for a single Web page often requires multiple interactions. One request and a response is required for each chunk of text in the document, plus at least one round for each image, sound, or any other module. The constant stream of bantering, however, is impractical for extraterrestrial messaging.

On Earth, a packet of data usually reaches its destination within a fraction of a second. The situation is otherwise in outer space.

Of the two planets closest to our own, one is hot and the other cold. Venus is a seething firepot whose orbit lies closer to the Sun. In contrast, Mars is a frigid rock which lies in the opposite direction, circling the starry hearth from a greater distance.

Between the pair of planets, the former is more forbidding. Venus has a solid mantle of clouds plus an atmosphere brimming with carbon dioxide. These two features have converted the planet into a greenhouse which traps the heat from the Sun. As a result, Venus is not merely warm but scalding hot. The world is no oasis, either for human or machine.

Mars, on the other hand, is a cold, dry and airless world. Despite its icy mien, the icon of war is more inviting than the goddess of love. For this reason, the red planet will become our first permanent outpost beyond the Moon.

Depending on the relative positions of the Earth and Mars as they twirl around the Sun, the distance between the two planets varies considerably. The gap ranges from a low of 56 million kilometers to a high in excess of 400 million km. At these distances, a message traveling at the speed of light takes anywhere from 3 to 20 minutes to span the gap.

Due to the inherent delay in communications between the two planets, the standard protocols for the Internet will be too awkward. A conversation in real time is out of the question.

An interplanetary version of the Internet has to adopt a different approach. Under the modified scheme, small packets of data need to be assembled into larger bundles, then sent as a composite package.[44] On the interplanetary Net, messaging is more akin to accelerated email than an online chat. The bundled scheme reduces the number of round-trip exchanges, thereby improving the timeliness of dispatches.

The protocols for the interworld Internet are designed to accommodate the delays due to vast distances among gateways in outer space. The same network scheme can be extended for communications between the Earth and its robotic envoys as they venture past the confines of the solar system. No doubt the architecture will also serve as a foundation for future spacecraft as they reach beyond our own galaxy and probe the vastness beyond.

Net Life

According to one notion of consciousness, the sense of self flows from the interplay of subatomic particles. A minute object such as an electron is difficult to pin down, since it has fuzzy features. Tiny particles obey physical laws which differ markedly from those we learned as infants.

An electron, for instance, can behave as if it were in two places at the same time. Another display of virtuosity is found in the property of tunneling, where an electron passes through a solid barrier even when it lacks the energy to do so. The same type of quantum effect allows a particle to leap across an empty gap without any effort at all. Spooky antics like these are the daily fare of physicists in a field called quantum mechanics.

Although the laws may seem alien to a sane mind, quantum effects serve as the foundation for a variety of practical devices in use today. An example lies in the scanning tunneling microscope, a device for scrutinizing a small object at the level of individual atoms on its surface.

The British mathematician and physicist Roger Penrose has argued for quantum effects as the wellspring of consciousness. In the realm of biology, the shape of a cell is bolstered by a network of thin filaments known as microtubules. Due to quantum properties, the protein molecules which comprise a microtubule may be linked to each other through a process of instantaneous action at a distance. In the entanglement of quantum particles, the condition of one object is affected immediately by the changing fortunes of a remote object.

For this reason, the behavior of particles in a collective can be coordinated through chains of entanglement. A pattern could shift in unison across a large array of proteins, resulting in coherent behavior which spans the width of a cell and perhaps even the brain as a whole. The aggregate patterns might then give rise to reasoning, reverie, and even consciousness itself. [45]

Our knowledge of quantum effects grew out of experiments with inanimate objects. In particular, the field of quantum physics rests on the study of elementary particles such as electrons and photons. Despite the physical origins of the theory, however, there is no reason to assume that quantum properties are the sole province of lifeless objects.

The basic element of synthetic intelligence is found in silicon, which forms the substrate for computer chips. The corresponding symbol for organic mentation lies in carbon, the backbone of cellular structures.

Carbon and silicon share a number of chemical properties, including the ability to form extensive chains or networks. The complex structures which result then serve as building blocks for purposive systems. Since silicon atoms can link together like their carbon cousins, the former could just as easily serve as the platform for life. In fact, scientists speculate that life elsewhere in the universe might be based on silicon rather than carbon.

The electronic behavior of a carbon atom is rooted in the 6-pack of protons in the nucleus. Surrounding the nuclear core is a hazy shell made up of six electrons.

An atom of silicon on the other hand, contains 14 protons in the nucleus. The positive charge due to the protons is balanced by the negative charge of electrons in the external shell. [46]

As far as we can tell, an electron or a proton is promiscuous: it does not care whether it forms part of an atom of carbon or silicon. For this reason, a particle which exhibits quantum traits in a carbon atom will be just as happy to act likewise in silicon. If quantum coherence gives rise to consciousness in a biological structure, it should do the same in a mechanical device.

Thanks to advances in nanotechnology, an assortment of molecular computers will be pressed into service over the next decade or so. A computer of atomic scale will have to rely on the behavior of individual atoms and their electrons. As we have seen, however, the ghostly properties of tiny objects could wreak havoc in a computing device. For instance, an electron might suddenly leap from one component to another without cause.

Despite the difficulties involved, a computer which relies on traditional forms of binary logic will have to rein in the flighty electrons by squelching their quantum clowning. Only then will the computer produce reliable results.

On the other hand, there is another path to the future. The radical approach is to turn a liability into an asset. More precisely, an electronic device could be designed to exploit quantum effects rather than suppress them. This is the tack taken by current efforts in quantum computing.

Since an electron can find itself in several states at once, it may be used as a slate to represent multiple objects at the same time. With fuzzy particles as building blocks, a quantum computer could embody scores of solutions simultaneously, then yield the proper answer to a query by selecting the corresponding reply. The process of favoring one condition over all the others, also known as *collapsing* to a state, happens all the time among quantum particles. Since a quantum computer could search a myriad paths in parallel, it can be orders of magnitude faster than a traditional machine.

By the eve of the millennium, rudimentary devices had already demonstrated the feasibility of computation based on quantum effects.[47] Machines of this ilk are likely to become practical devices over the next decade.

A nanoscale device has to accommodate quantum effects. In fact, a quantum computer could not operate without the whimsical streak in minute particles. If quantum entanglement, or any other process, can give rise to consciousness in an organic brain, then it ought to do likewise in an inorganic one.

The preceding argument has focused on machines made of minerals. A different strain of computers will grow out of organic molecules. This type of wetware will emerge from current efforts in protein computation.[48] Organic computers employ principles of self-organization, where individual molecules arrange themselves as required for a task. This is the same principle of information processing involved in the birth, repair or regulation of an ordinary cell in living tissue.

An organic computer of this form might look different from an animal or a human. A civilized computer has no need for tails to swing from trees nor teeth to sink into prey. Even so, the principles behind their operation will be the same as those for living beings.

The convergence of the biological and the mechanical is also arising from another direction. The years to come will witness direct links between people and machines. A simple example is a hybrid pacemaker for the heart: a device which runs on energy from biochemical pathways, powered much like any natural organ. A novel pacemaker, grown artificially in a pool of organic and inorganic molecules, could incorporate a mobile channel to the Net. The device would then issue a prompt alarm in case of cardiac failure. In this scenario, which is organic and which not? Which is part of the Net and which not? There is no line which separates the device from the organ, nor the individual from the collective.

The years ahead will also bring conscious links between people and the Net. Changes in thought affect the frequency and intensity of waves from particular regions of the brain. Based on this phenomenon, sensors connected to the Web will be able to detect the type and strength of radiation from specific sites on the brain.

At first, the readings will be crude. For instance, a tracker might be sensitive enough only to differentiate between serenity and agitation, with the attendant implications for a smart house catering to its owner's moods. In due course, the sensors will be sufficiently refined to distinguish between pensiveness and worry, or the desire to learn about daisies rather than daffodils. A digital aide could then respond accordingly.

As noted earlier, increasing numbers of people will choose to obtain implants to augment their memory or to boost processing speed. A related accessory is a communication device to receive messages directly from the Net. With a digital prosthetic, the flow of information need not be restricted to the speed of talking, reading, or viewing. Instead, data can be acquired at the speed of thought - or even faster, by downloading files directly onto a memory chip without conscious intervention.

The groundwork is then laid for telepathy, where thinking is sufficient to send or receive messages by a simple act of will. At first, communicating via thought will be a clunky version of telepathy. A message could be conveyed from one person to a sensor tied to the Net, then relayed to a base station before the final step of delivery to the intended recipient. Even this mode of interaction would represent an improvement on current channels for videoconferencing or dealing with household robots.

Ultimately, messaging between two parties might be instantaneous. Through quantum entanglement, the condition of a particle can immediately affect the state of a remote object. In that case, a thought forming in one person's mind could be conveyed in some fashion to a receiver in another person's implant. A suitable interpreter on the receiver might then make sense of the abstruse changes in pattern.

As the nexus for all sorts of communication, the Net will be privy to much of the content and activity at each node in the system. Once the network learns to synthesize information and to select its own mode of growth, it becomes more than a passive infrastructure. The Net then acquires the wherewithal to reach beyond its mechanical origins.

Somewhere down the road, the network is likely to grow into the most sentient entity in our corner of the cosmos. The capacity for autonomous evolution will mark the last major transition of the Net over the foreseeable future. The fourth generation of the Internet should begin around the mid-century mark, as indicated in Table 7.2.

Table 7.2. Living Net. The fourth generation of the Internet will begin around 2050.

Feature	Sample Application
Mental input	Partial telepathy via brain waves
Web life	Agents which can live and evolve indefinitely within the Net
Sentient Net	Consciousness of the network as a whole
Extragalactic Web	Intergalactic spacecraft

If history is any indication, the spirit of exploration will not die within the confines of our own galaxy. Looking ahead into the twilight of the 21st century, we can easily envision spacecraft which cast off on journeys to neighboring galaxies. The robotic probes may take millennia to complete their mission, but they could send back occasional reports in the interim. The information acquired in transit should help to clarify the nature of the universe: the origin, structure and fate of all the worlds.

The age of the sentient Net could endure indefinitely in the absence of natural cataclysms or artificial catastrophes. It would seem inevitable, however, for breakouts to occur from time to time.

If the yen for adventure continues to thrive, science will uncover new laws beyond our ken today. At the dawn of the millennium, we cannot yet fathom the panorama of transcendent events which await our kind on the distant horizon.

On the other hand, we can be confident of one thing. The creative minds, both physical and virtual, which break down the frontiers will make full use of the knowledge cached in the Net all over the Earth and in the heavens above.

Choosing a Lifestyle

Some people will choose to stay connected to the Net at all hours of the day and night. The adherents will find stimulation in the kaleidoscope of knowledge and sensory treats offered by the nexus.

For individuals used to the vista of outdoor life or the bustle of a modern town, the darkness and silence of a cellar can be frightening. A long stretch of isolation is enough to drive a sane person up a wall and over the edge.

In a similar way, a habitué of cyberspace is likely to find banishment from its borders to be a cruel and unusual punishment. Some folks will find fulfillment only in the midst of the effervescence and fellowship which is always at hand on the Web.

At the other end of sociality, individuals with a fierce sense of independence will avoid the Net like a blight. Those who long for the past or revel in quiet contemplation will shun the network and the wares on offer. Among the rejectors, a number of souls will be die-hard hermits. Yet others will be reluctant users who tap into the nexus only when necessary: to obtain a morsel of data or to conduct an electronic transaction.

On the whole, denizens of the digital society will choose a lifestyle between the extremes of complete absorption and total exile. The majority may well monitor activity on the Net in background mode, much as their predecessors would listen to music while driving or leave the television running during a conversation. Then depending on her needs of the moment, a Netizen might savor the parade of online content with full or partial engagement.

The level of interaction is likely to vary over the course of the day, from full immersion in a virtual world at one end of the spectrum to complete isolation at the other. In sum, the nature and scope of engagement in the nexus will vary from one person to another and from one instant to the next.

Summary

The Internet was born of military needs during the Cold War. As fate would have it, the Net came into existence during the same era that mankind reached for the Moon.

The World Wide Web brought the Internet into the mainstream of the informatic society. The Net came to serve as a storehouse for all sorts of information and a conduit for the free flow of communications. With the universality of standards and the openness of the architecture, the network became a force for cohesion and cooperation among the peoples of the world.

The Net has spawned nomadic robots which scour the Web on behalf of human principals. The platform also harbors agents which synthesize knowledge from inert data and learn to improve their performance with experience.

The network has come to serve as the main stage for exhibiting creativity of all types. The modes of innovation range from virtual art and online adventure to scientific collaboration and electronic commerce.

Over the long run, the software technology of evolutionary systems will play a defining role. Today the Net is a cradle for the first generation of digital entities with the capacity to evolve on their own. Armed with only a mission profile and a critical mass of code, these creatures of the Web adapt from one generation to the next using the principles of population genetics.

The Net is turning into a nexus for all knowledge and communication among people as well as machines. The network is now only a tool for sentient users. Yet the matrix is destined some day to evolve a sentience of its own.

Barring any catastrophes along the way, this child of humanity will in time convey our message to the stars. As the archive of knowledge, the platform for culture, and the conduit for all action, the Net will turn out to be the centerpiece of our contribution to posterity.

About the Author

Steven Kim is a specialist in technical innovation and Internet media. As a professor at MIT in the 1980s, he received a Presidential Young Investigator award by the U.S. National Science Foundation in recognition of his original research activities. In his current role as Distinguished Professor at Sookmyung University, he grapples with the jigsaw of innovation in the digital society.

Appendix A

Multimedia on the Net

This appendix presents a tutorial on basic concepts and uses of multimedia on the Internet. The technical overview complements the presentation in Chapter 2, while the applications supplement the other chapters. The material here may be scanned as an orientation to the trunk of the book, or as a review after reading the text.

$$\boxed{\text{Outline}}$$

- ● Introduction
- ● Internet
- ● Virtual Reality
- ● Intelligent Web
- ● Applications
- ● Expanding Directions
- ● Conclusion

INTRODUCTION

Motivation for Multimedia

● Comprehension
  ■ "A picture is worth a thousand words."

● Attention / Retention
  ■ Sight, sound & motion
    ◆ Hold the user's attention & enhance recall compared to a single sensory mode.
  ■ Possibility of interactivity
    ◆ Active involvement of user rather than passive viewing.

Types of Media

● Text
● Graphics
● Image
● Animation
● Audio
● Video

INTERNET

● Internet = a network of networks using a common set of standards.

● Advantages

- ■ Decentralized architecture
  - ◆ Eliminates need for centralized control
- ■ Open software platforms using TCP/IP standards
  - ◆ Diverse hardware
- ■ Robustness
  - ◆ Fault tolerance: dynamic routing of messages by packet switching

- ● First generation tools
  - ■ SMTP = protocol for email
  - ■ FTP = File Transfer Protocol
  - ■ Telnet for remote interactive sessions
  - ■ Gopher for searching remote databases

- ● Second generation tool
  - ■ World Wide Web: supports hypermedia documents

- ● Reasons for popularity of Internet
  - ■ Open standards: easy to establish connectivity
  - ■ Tradition of liberal information exchange
  - ■ Little or no direct cost to individual users
  - ■ Fault tolerance
    - ◆ Lack of centralized control
    - ◆ Dynamic routing bypasses links which are inoperative or heavily loaded
  - ■ Snowball effect: myriads of users, and growing rapidly.

- ● Host = a computer connected to the Internet
  - ■ Internet Protocol (IP) Number = unique identifier for each host.

● Gateway = a host which connects a proprietary network to the Internet.

● Router = a network device which conveys a data packet to the next host, depending on the identity of destination host and current status of the network in the neighboring region.

World Wide Web
Protocols

● World Wide Web (WWW) = a virtual network of documents residing on Internet hosts & employing the HTTP standard.
● HTTP (HyperText Transfer Protocol) = a standard for exchanging documents.
● URL (Uniform/Universal Resource Locator) = a standard for identifying the location of documents.
● HTML (HyperText Markup Language) = a standard for formatting multimedia documents & providing hypertext links to other items.

VIRTUAL REALITY

Simulated Worlds

● Virtual Reality (VR) = a realistic environment simulated by computer

● Sensory modes
  ■ Vision
      ◆ 3-dimensional (3D); full realism through stereoscopic projections.
      ◆ Integration of materials for presentation to user

- ● E.g. 3D-goggles; direct projection of low-power beam into each eye.
    - ◆ Spatial distribution
        - ● E.g. Perspective; casting shadows; changing rendered shapes according to vantage point ("moving camera").
- ■ Touch
    - ◆ Data glove—>feeling of resistance on user's hands.

- ■ Sound
    - ◆ Stereophonic
- ■ Olfaction
    - ◆ No smells yet on the Net
- ■ Taste
    - ◆ None yet

- ● Simulation of real world
    - ■ Collision
        - ◆ E.g. Can't walk through walls.
    - ■ Forces
        - ◆ E.g. Subject to gravitational pull

- ● Standards
    - ■ Virtual Reality Modeling Language (VRML)
    - ■ VRML97 = official version of a proposed draft called VRML 2.0
    - ■ Java 3D: faster than VRML
    - ■ *Viewpoint* standard permits real-time rendering
        - ◆ E.g. *Atmosphere* toolkit by Adobe produces models in Viewpoint format.

Virtual Reality Modeling Language

● Virtual Reality Modeling Language (VRML) = a scene description language
—> implement VR on the World Wide Web.
● Browser = software which interprets (not compiles) a VRML file.

● Rendering = generating a scene on the display screen.

- ■ Rendering software
- ■ Live 3D from Netscape
- ■ Cosmo Player from Silicon Graphics.
- ■ Etc.

Real-time, Online 3D

● Atmosphere = software to create & explore virtual worlds
- ■ Introduced in 2001 by Adobe
- ■ Comprises 3 components
  - ◆ *Builder* creates virtual spaces using Viewpoint format
  - ◆ *Player* is the browser for rendering a virtual world
  - ◆ *Community Server* hosts virtual worlds for multiuser interaction

● Adobe Systems = a vendor of content development tools
- ■ www.adobe.com
- ■ Founded in 1982
- ■ Based in San Jose, California.

Extensible 3D on the Web

- X3D = eXtensible standard for 3D on the Web
  - ■ Project launched in 2001 by Web 3D, a consortium (web3d.org) of vendors
  - ■ Next generation of VRML
  - ■ Follows XML standards
  - ■ Can view virtual worlds on wired or mobile screens

- Xj3D = a browser developed by Web 3D Consortium
  - ■ Compatible with VRML and Java 3D
  - ■ Java 3D = set of procedures to handle 3D objects in Java language
    - ◆ Developed by Sun Microsystems

INTELLIGENT WEB

Meaningful Content in Documents

- XML = eXensible Markup Language
  - ■ Metalevel format for creating targeted languages for use in accounting, business, chemistry, dentistry, and so on.
  - ■ Users can create tags to denote whether an item of data such as "37" denotes the age of a patient, his room number, parking slot, or whatever.

Meaningful Content on the Web

- Semantic Web = a project to enable software to understand the nature of content on the Net
  - ■ An activity of the World Wide Web Consortium (W3C): www.w3.org
  - ■ Relies on XML, RDF, and URI

- Resource Description Framework (RDF)
  - ■ Encodes statements in the form S-R-O, where S is the subject, R the relationship, and O the object
  - ■ E.g. S = "Alex"
    R = "is the father of"
    O = "Jane"

- Uniform Resource Identifier (URI)
  - ■ An item which specifies each subject, relationship, or object
  - ■ Each URI is defined at some node on the Web
  - ■ Uniform Resource Locator (URL) is a common subtype of URI

$$\boxed{\text{APPLICATIONS}}$$

Online Entertainment

- Shockwave.com = a division of Macromedia Inc., based in San Francisco.
  - ■ Interactive entertainment for online or offline play.
  - ■ Categories include games, cartoons, comics, music, etc.
  - ■ www.shockwave.com

Virtual Fashion Model

- Webbie Tookay ("Web 2K") = 17-year-old cyber model developed for "Elite Illusion 2K"
  - ■ Company is a joint venture between Elite Models & Illusion 2K of Brazil.
  - ■ Model is designed for appearances on TV ads, Websites, games, etc.

■   www.illusion2k.com

Avatars

●   Avatar = an online representative of a user.

●   Contact Consortium = a forum for virtual reality on the Net.
   ■   Each user is represented by an avatar
   ■   Netizens can learn, play, and interact in virtual worlds
   ■   www.ccon.org

Digital Cinema

●   Digital movies at theaters.
   ■   Digital projectors manipulate red, green & blue dots.
      ◆   Similar to TV screen.
   ■   First used in 1999 for *Stars Wars: Phantom Menace* at cinemas in NY and LA.
   ■   www.cinedc.com

Online Conferencing

●   Stadium = a cyber environment for staging large-scale live events with many participants or spectators.
   ■   Under development since 1995 at the Knowledge Media Institute of the Open University in the UK.
   ■   Technologies include Java, synchronized audio and other multimedia.
   ■   Participants can provide feedback.
      ◆   E.g. Push buttons for "applause" or "laughter".
   ■   kmi.open.ac.uk

Business Simulation

- Powersim = a vendor of software for simulations: scenario planning, employee training, etc.
    - Head office in Reston, Virginia.
    - Simulation software can be linked to ERP and other packages.
    - Private firm whose investors include SAP.
    - www.powersim.com

- Applications
    - British Petroleum used software to reduce bottlenecks in its supply chain.
    - Bosch Automotive improved its manufacturing process.
    - Anderson Consulting worked with a client to improve managerial processes and worker motivation.

Web Television

- AOL TV = a service for Web TV by America Online.
    - Launched in summer 2000.
    - Offers several Net sites, plus email.
    - www.aoltv.com

- Ultimate TV = a similar service by Microsoft.
    - Replacement for Web TV, a Silicon Valley startup purchased by Microsoft for $425 million in 1997.
    - Offers Net access.
    - Personal Video Recorder (PVR): user can select programs to record at the touch of a button.

Web TV by Satellite

- Speedcast = a venture firm which offers TV to Internet service providers and end users.
  - 1999: Established in Hong Kong.
  - Service includes channels from Bloomberg TV, Yahoo Broadcast, etc.
  - Broadband satellite transmission bypasses intercity Internet traffic on the ground.
  - Satellite footprint covers all of Asia, from Japan to Egypt.
  - Revenues from advertising, plus subscription fees eventually.
  - www.speedcast.com

EXPANDING DIRECTIONS

- Smart agents

- Mobile media

- Virtual communities

Customer Service Agent

- LucasArts
  - Game vendor in San Rafael, California.
  - www.lucasarts.com

- Users interact with a character named Yoda
  - Natural language interface.
  - About 1,000 queries/day.
  - Handles the work of 33 human "customer service reps".

Wireless Internet

- Wireless Application/Access Protocol (WAP) = a standard for Web services using mobile devices
  - ■ Wireless Markup Language (WML) = a mobile version of HTML
  - ■ WMLScript = a mobile version of JavaScript

- WAP Forum = an industry consortium to promote WAP

- Compact HTML (CHTML) = a mobile version of HTML used by NTT DoCoMo of Japan

Mobile Video

- PacketVideo = a vendor of utilities to send video to mobile devices
  - ■ Located in San Diego, California.
  - ■ Investors include Sony, Reuters, Intel, Qualcomm.

- Technology
  - ■ Initial rate of 5 frames per second; designed to increase with 3G wireless technology.
  - ■ Uses MPEG-4 format.

- Applications
  - ■ Parents can watch toddlers at home.
  - ■ Viewers can preview a movie before ordering it.
  - ■ Surfers can watch news.

Communication among Heterogeneous Devices

● Bluetooth = a standard to permit wireless devices to communicate with each other through infrared beams.

■ Named after a Danish king who brought together warring tribes.

● Symbian = an example of a Bluetooth alliance.

■ Initiated in 1998 by Psion of UK, joining with Ericsson & Nokia.

■ EPOC = operating system for palmtop organizers made by Psion.

● A de facto standard for smart phones.

■ 1999: alliance joined by Motorola, NTT DoCoMo, Sun Microsystems & Matsushita.

■ Alliance produces 85% of mobile phones worldwide.

■ EPOC can run Java programs.

A Universal Operating System?

● Windows CE = a slimmer version of Windows operating system by Microsoft.

■ Microsoft's alliance:

◆ Firm owns part of Nextel, a US network operator.

◆ Slated to develop wireless services for Qualcomm (US developer of CDMA), and British Telecom.

◆ Windows CE is used in smart phones by Philips, Panasonic, Acer, etc.

■   Windows CE is designed to run a variety of devices, including set-top boxes for cable TV.
—> Operating system may be too clunky for mobile phones.

Property Ownership
in Cyberspace

● Virtual property has real value.
  ■   Persistence: an online object exists independently of users.

● *Lineage: Blood Throne*
  ■   Multiuser, 3D adventure game, developed by NCSoft of Korea.
  ■   Characters' actions are displayed in real time:
     ◆   Move, speak, fight, etc.
  ■   Players can collude against other players.
  ■   Players can trade or sell weapons on Net.
     ◆   Weapons have sold for over $2,000.
     ◆   Thefts of weapons occur in cyberspace.
     —> Can a thief be prosecuted in real space?
     ◆   lineage.co.kr

$$\boxed{\text{CONCLUSION}}$$

● Multimedia and virtual reality can support operations of the host firm plus those of customers, suppliers, and other stakeholders.
  ■   Productivity
  ■   Effectiveness

● Merits of online media.

   ■ Multimedia items convey information more quickly compared to a uni-modal system, e.g. text or audio alone.

   ■ Cyberspace offers global reach.

   ■ Friendly aides increase efficiency for the user.

   ■ Smart agents can outperform humans.

Appendix B

Designing a Digital Strategy

For several decades beginning in the 1960s, organizations around the world invested heavily in information technology. Unfortunately, both casual observation and formal scrutiny at the time usually failed to detect any impact on productivity.

Around 1990, however, a versatile set of tools began to fulfill the promise of informatics, a grail which had eluded digital advocates in the past. Among the ascendant motifs on the scene, the primary colors were to be found in open standards, multimedia, and data mining.

A foundation for the new initiative was the Internet and its attendant technologies. In the sphere of multimedia platforms, the key lay in the interlace of hypertext, audio, and video within the World Wide Web. Further, the deployment of machine learning led to automated methods for discovering knowledge from raw data.

This appendix explores a variety of critical issues in developing a virtual enterprise based on these themes. Moreover, a toolkit of practical rules covers the construction of a digital strategy for the knowledge based organization.

Developing a Net Strategy

All too often, disparate groups within an enterprise build systems whose efficacy is procured at the expense of other divisions. This can occur, for instance, when a group implements a bland package whose low cost fulfills short-term targets from a financial viewpoint. However, the cheap solution may well present compatibility problems with neighboring systems and even hinder future projects by the hosting division itself.

For these reasons, a rational strategy has to take account of the ultimate mission of the entire enterprise. The collective objectives may range from customer service and employee development to corporate earnings and societal contribution.

At the same time, the planning effort must also take pains to avoid unintended side effects. To illustrate, a corporate policy might specify a single type of operating system such as Unix or Windows across the entire organization. But in the current age of open standards, such a constraint is likely to shackle every division without any benefit in overall compatibility or cost reduction.

To rent a phrase, mindless conformity is the hobgoblin of mediocrity. In fact, the diversity of digital platforms can be a virtue under the right circumstances. A case in point lies in the use of Macintosh computers within product development groups at IBM, the ancestral home of the PC. Within the framework of open standards, variety is a virtue rather than a vice.

Among the outlying divisions of innumerable enterprises, a popular image of corporate headquarters is a den of busybodies. The gnomes at headquarters are regarded in the periphery as tormentors rather than partners in the quest to cyberize the organization.

Against this backdrop, the policy makers at the center have to ensure that their efforts do in fact have a positive rather than negative impact.

Some safe rules of conduct for the central office in molding an informatic policy are as follows.

- Disseminate background information on advancing technologies which may impact strategic plans for the entire corporation as well as specific divisions.
- Conduct benchmarking studies of applications both within the firm and in external organizations.
- Proffer mostly guidelines and suggestions rather than rigid fiats.
- Avoid micro-management of the operating divisions.

To ensure hearty collaboration from the operating groups, it is not enough for the head office to simply behave in a helpful fashion. Rather, to elicit more than grudging support from the field, the center has to promote the image as well as the reality of lending a helpful hand. This requires proper communications through the intranet and other channels, as well as establishing a history of good deeds.

Core Principles. An informatic policy should build on a foundation of guiding principles. In this vein, the basics relate to the notions of open architecture, failure containment, and continuous innovation.

In the age of the Net, it is a straightforward matter to design a digital system based on universal standards. This leads to the first of the Core Principles for an informatic policy.

- All systems, comprising both hardware and software units, should conform to open standards.

The adoption of generic formats allows for the use of off-the-shelf products, resulting in higher reliability and lower cost. In addition, obsolete modules can be upgraded with minimal disturbance to legacy systems.

An unexpected glitch in one package should not hamper the operation of another system. To this end, information systems should be modular to ensure the containment of a breakdown.

● Where feasible, the failure of an existing system or a new project should not materially affect other systems, either within the same division or elsewhere.

For instance, the collapse of a reporting module in the marketing division should not cripple operations in the finance department.

An informatic system begins to obsolesce as soon as it is completed. Consequently, a strategy of continual learning and upgrading is essential.

● Information technology should be adopted on a continuing basis to enhance the effectiveness and efficiency of business processes.

The need for steady innovation gives rise to a number of policy guidelines. A couple of implications spring from the foregoing principle.

● **Corollary 1.** Each division and department should undertake any project which is justified by the expected benefits and costs.

With astonishing frequency, managers run autonomous fiefs and try to foil advances in adjoining groups. A standard excuse for the parry is that each department should await the completion of a grand unified plan which covers the entire enterprise and its myriad divisions.

In an age of rapid progress, grandiose blueprints never reach completion. Rather, they begin to look antiquated even before the ink is dry. Meanwhile, an enterprise which tolerates such paralyzing tactics eventually finds itself tottering toward a state of terminal repose.

● **Corollary 2.** A record of 100% successes indicates insufficient risk taking. A failed project should be accepted as a useful lesson rather than a source of embarrassment, as long as the project had satisfied the Core Principles plus Corollary 1.

The origin of the second corollary above lies in the risky nature of innovations. For pioneers, failure is a constant companion. However, honest mistakes also sow the seeds of future success.[49]

Every organization needs to promote creativity despite the risks entailed. To this end, a number of leading companies award prizes at an annual ceremony to celebrate exemplary failures as well as notable successes. All other organizations would benefit from a similar tradition.

Target Levels for Digital Applications

Digital technology can support an enterprise at a variety of informatic levels. One way to classify the level of application lies in the triad of data, information, and knowledge.

The *data level* refers to the acquisition, storage and manipulation of elementary facts or symbols. Examples of applications at the lowest level are as follows.

● Automated data entry, as illustrated by voice recognition to eliminate typing.
● A data warehouse to provide a unified view of activity across the entire organization.

The *information level* applies to the use of data for routine operations. The decision maker may be located on the internal side of the corporate boundary, as exemplified by an employee or an advisor; or on the external side, as in the case of a customer or supplier. Instances of applications at the information layer are found in the following.

- An intranet or extranet to disseminate information quickly, and to reduce operating costs.
- Multimedia to alleviate the burden of information overload for decision makers.

Digital systems at the *knowledge level* address ad hoc decisions which affect policy or strategy in a substantive way. The prime example of a technology which caters to this level lies in data mining. Sample applications in this group are found in the forecast of economic growth, prediction of consumer behavior, or assessment of political risk. With the help of knowledge level systems, a decision maker can analyze the internal environment to identify opportunities for process improvement as well as the external milieu for strategy formulation.

Digital Policy

Against the backdrop of bolting technologies and grueling competition, a coherent strategy for cyberization is crucial for survival. The strategic plan must also be fortified by a rational policy which governs routine operations.

This section presents a number of guidelines for creating a competitive plan. The recommendations relate to two major themes: people and processes. The former category relates to the hiring, retention and empowering of personnel. The latter group involves the creation or refinement of a planning process for cyberization.

In crafting a digital policy, the keystone lies in proper *recognition* of the importance of informatics.

● Assign the post of a Chief Informatic Officer (CIO) at a senior executive level.
● Pursue a policy of perpetual benchmarking and pay the market rate for all digital specialists.

These are obvious prerequisites for nurturing a strong informatic team, but the obvious is at times ignored. For instance, all companies proclaim their desire to attract top-notch cyberians; but many trailing firms are unwilling to offer competitive wages. Since deeds speak louder than words, potential employees take notice and decide with their feet by heading for the competition.

Every organization should embrace a systematic approach to enhancing its human capital. To this end, one visible tactic is to establish an *Internet Education Office* to update all employees' skills on a continuing basis. Although the details will vary from one firm to the next, several examples will illustrate the role of this office.

● Sponsoring a lecture series on *Frontiers in Cyberspace*, addressing timely topics in technical trends as well as practical case studies. This is a cost-effective way to educate employees.
   ◆ Lectures may be scheduled on a monthly basis at first, then more frequently after a successful trial period.
   ◆ To appeal to non-technical personnel, a good fraction of the lectures should address strategic issues for a managerial audience.
● Offering a series of training programs on informatic subjects for all employees.
   ◆ Each course may be modular, comprising perhaps half a day per week for a month or two.

- ◆ Subjects can be offered on diverse topics such as intranets, extranets, data mining, digital marketing, multimedia systems, warehousing, forecasting tools, and so on.
- ◆ Each employee could be required to earn a minimum number of credit hours every year.
- ● Evaluating and recommending a series of friendly tools which end-users can employ to generate customized reports. The tools should require no programming by the user.
- ● Encouraging employees to join professional associations and participate in conferences on informatics.

After every educational event, each attendee should be solicited for comments and suggestions for future topics, speakers, or activities.

As indicated earlier, the hallmark of leadership is continuous innovation. This should be a central theme in every staff meeting each week at all levels of the organization. The participants should be encouraged to ask questions such as the following.

- ● "How can we exploit emerging tools and concepts to generate new products, expand markets, and boost efficiency?"
- ● "What is the best way to further automate data collection and processing activities?"
- ● "How can we enhance responsiveness to changing markets by improving extranets with customers and suppliers as well as intermediaries such as banks and outsourcing partners?"

Since digital technology continues to trot ahead, chasing after it to secure competitive advantage is a never-ending task.

A vanguard organization has to establish a formal planning process for cyberization and improve the mechanism on a regular basis.

- Headquarters should properly assume responsibility for the *macrolevel* strategy for the entire organization.
- Every division has to take charge of its own *mesolevel* strategy.
- Each department is responsible for the *microlevel* strategy.
- Corporate headquarters and each division should make plans for a sequence of planning horizons: 1 year, 2 years, and 5 years at a minimum.
- As with most strategic plans, the digital agenda should be developed multilaterally, as a joint effort among headquarters and the operating groups.
- The long-range strategy should be evergreen: rolling 5-year plans, revised each year.

With the trend toward outsourcing, routine activities such as accounting are often delegated to external providers. Extramural support for knowledge level work is even more acute when high-level skills are unavailable within the firm.

Most organizations would profit from the judicious use of consultants and advisors to help develop systems and to transfer skills. The advisors may assume primary responsibility for the overall design of a digital system. Meanwhile, the main responsibility for system implementation, including programming, can be discharged by the host organization.

Unfortunately, the manager in charge of a project often selects one consultant or advisor over other contenders based on the policy of "Cover your rump": engage a personality with a household name. In that case, even if the swami produces tepid results, the manager responsible can evade reproof.

A vintage name, however, is a reliable source for only one type of knowledge. An old-timer, having visited many firms over the years, is a storehouse of data on benchmark operations.

On the downside, a surfeit of popularity has its pitfalls. A guru who spends all his time delivering a worn spiel has little time to analyze subtle developments in neighboring realms. With unsettling frequency, a radical technology or practice can sneak up on a complacent player and supplant the rules of the game at a single stroke.

In selecting a consultant, an excessive reliance on public acclaim is the way to win bygone battles rather than future wars. A firm at the leading edge has to assess its needs thoughtfully, then seek out advice to match from diverse sources.

Fame plays a differential role for the vendor and the consumer. Enhancing a brand is a source of strength for a seller. In contrast, thraldom to a brand in the face of better alternatives is a sign of weakness for a buyer. A discerning manager has to keep the distinction in mind as he scours the globe for a consultant or any other source of supply.

Amidst the turmoil wrought by digital technology, an enterprising firm has to take proactive steps to ensure prosperity. For a thorough discussion of the issues, only a veritable library of tomes could do justice; and each book would begin to show its age on the day of publication.

Although a comprehensive list of actions is impractical, the alternative here is to offer a number of generic guidelines. A resourceful firm could do worse than to embrace the following tactics.

- Create a *vanguard team* in each division to consider high-level business objectives and the potential role of advanced informatics. Examples of techniques and their applications include the following.
  - ◆ Knowledge based tools for long-term forecasting.
  - ◆ Customer targeting to improve marketing efficacy.
  - ◆ Risk management systems to reduce currency exposure in cash positions.

- Commission a *security team* with representatives from each division to examine and recommend security measures. Some core topics for consideration:
  - ◆ Identification of users to thwart impersonation.
  - ◆ Authorization to allow only approved activities by a particular user.
  - ◆ Encryption of sensitive data.
- Top management should cultivate a state of "cybermind" in themselves and other employees.
  - ◆ Hold regular jam sessions with their staff on new ways of using electronic tools to raise revenues, slash costs, and so on. Each event should include line managers as well as functional staff (finance, marketing, etc.) and digital specialists. The moderator for the session could be a spirited employee or an experienced outsider.
  - ◆ Personally attend as many talks as possible in the informatic lecture series.
  - ◆ Suggest additional capabilities for an executive information system (EIS) as part of the strategic plan for cyberization each year.

An executive might suggest a new feature in an EIS and later draw on its capabilities either directly or indirectly. In the latter case, the system may be operated on a routine basis by an aide rather than the executive personally.

The need for a human assistant, however, will only be temporary. By the second decade of the 21st century, any user will be able to access the wealth of resources on the Web by talking to digital agents which respond through speech, graphics, and video.

Summary

The growth of electronic commerce stems from digital systems to automate the capture of information, respond to unforeseen crises, and capitalize on environmental changes. For many organizations, Net technology is the flagship in the campaign to acquire or bolster competitive advantage.

All over the globe, cyberization is moving forward with gathering speed. To survive the tremors and the ensuing shakedown, each enterprise has to emplace a nimble array of digital vehicles for maneuvering on shifty ground.

Unfortunately, experience has shown that large-scale projects in all sorts of industries tend to fall short of expectations. For instance, estimates of the failure rate of projects in business process reengineering usually range from 50 to 70 percent.

To attain its full potential, an informatic system requires a good measure of process reengineering at the outset. For this reason, a sizable project is more susceptible to disappointment than is commonly acknowledged.

Over the past few decades, extensive studies in the field have underscored the importance of aligning a digital system with the cultural environment of the organization. In particular, employees will shun software which requires an onerous adjustment in procedures, whether in the learning or operating phase.

Perhaps more importantly, a virtual system affects the availability and flow of data, thereby disturbing power structures. This leads to underwhelming levels of cooperation in constructing and/or operating the system, ultimately leading to failed expectations. For a vital project, it is therefore crucial to elicit the wholehearted cooperation of all stakeholders, from the chief executive to the front-line employee.

This appendix has explored a number of principles which appear to be requisites for the success of a program for cyberization. The lessons have been distilled from decades of experience in implementing digital systems in diverse industries.

Even so, there is no magic potion for leadership: the basic recipe can only serve as a starting point for brewing a virtual strategy. The challenge and opportunity for each enterprise is to concoct a winning plan in accord with its own circumstances.

Appendix C

Education in Cyberspace

The rapid development of the Web has led to innovations in the practice of science, business, and other fields. A celebrated feature of the Internet is its treasury of data and documents. Given this resource, one of the most promising applications of the Web lies in education.[50]

The potential of computer networks to revolutionize education has been widely acclaimed. Unfortunately, much like the earlier technologies of television and film, the envisioned promise of computer networks has remained largely unfulfilled.[51]

The Web provides a colorful window into cyberspace through text, images, audio, and video. At the dawn of the 21st century, these capabilities were still poorly utilized in cyberia. Although the user could switch from one Web page to another through hypertext links, she remained largely a spectator. The experience was not much different from channel surfing on a television set.

Today the Net is the global platform for a new generation of educational resources through interactive media. Online documents can integrate images, video, animation, and text to provide a rich sensory environment. A dynamic presentation in concert with the active involvement of the user can make the learning experience more comprehensible, enjoyable, and memorable.

This appendix explores a number of issues behind the use of multimedia on the Web, presents a clutch of pioneering sites, and explores the promise of digital capabilities. To clarify the issues, the discussion focuses on initiatives in mathematics education. Despite the focus of the case study, the interactive concepts and design principles are applicable to other realms of formal or ad hoc instruction. The concluding section presents some generalizations plus directions for the future.

Trends and Tools on the Web

All over the globe, diverse forms of information are being created, captured, or converted into digital form. Documents are generated digitally on personal computers while sales transactions are recorded with scanners at check-out counters, and works of art are zapped into electronic images. Further, the linkage of previously isolated computers has led to the accessibility of both public and private information through online networks.

To an increasing extent, computer networks permeate everyday life at school, home and office. For this reason, the information highway is a ubiquitous platform for learning on demand.

The Internet allows for the fusion of multiple media ranging from text to video. In addition, the technology offers unprecedented depth through the ability to depict 3-dimensional worlds.

The universal standard for displaying information online is the HyperText Markup Language (HTML), which specifies how information should be presented on a 2-D screen. A complementary standard lies in the Java programming language. Java is a general-purpose language which can depict objects within an HTML document or control other objects on a network. For instance, an applet is a small program written in Java which might be used for, say, controlling the animation of a dog running across a 2-D scene whose overall structure is specified in HTML. In an analogous way, Java can be used to process information or specify complex relationships among objects in a 3-D world.

The conventions of HTML and Java offer a way to present information to students through dynamic media. HTML can be used to lay out the 2-D presentation on the screen. Meanwhile Java is used to control behaviors within and between the following interfaces: the 2-D screen, the simulated world within, and real-time interactions with the user.

Pioneering Systems

At the turn of the millennium, a search of the Net for content on mathematics instruction yielded a small set of progressive examples. A list of exemplary Websites is identified in Table C.1. The chart presents an evaluation of strengths and limitations, followed by some ideas for improving each site.

In a similar way, a variety of programs or software packages for mathematics education was sought. The harvest of notable programs is presented in Table C.2.

Table C.1. A collection of exemplary Websites for mathematics education.

Site name	URL	Strengths	Limitations	Recommendations
MathDEN	www3.actden.com/ math_den	Clean screen design. Good navigation. Rich content. Attractive image icon.	Stale site: infrequent updates. Long download times. Only text and 2D graphics.	Use not only text and 2D graphics but also audio, animation & other multimedia.
Math Education	pegasus.cc.ucf.edu/ ~mathed/home.html	Fast download. Exercises at various levels of difficulty. "Problem of the week" contest: offers motivation.	Boring screen design. No navigation icon.	Improve user navigation aids. Employ multimedia. Create interesting screen design.
Mathematics Center	www.eduplace.com/ math	Esthetic design. Fast loading. Good hyperlinks. Easy navigational control. Review of last problem & answer.	Inefficient screen layout. Response by email may be a hurdle for kids. Inconsistent site design.	For each basic program, provide different versions for various expertise levels. Consider skill level of user. Offer additional problems & learning materials.
Kidspsych	www.kidspsych.org	Highly interactive. Effective use of multimedia. Good user interface.	Small set of programs.	Increase diversity of programs.
SOS MATHematics	www.sosmath.com/ index.html	Abundant stock of materials. Immediate feedback. Systematic explanation. Depth of math instruction.	Poor motivational factor. Material is mostly text. Excessive scrolling required. Poor navigation.	Use multimedia. Improve esthetics. Split long documents into several smaller ones.

Table C.2. A list of notable programs for mathematics education on the Web.

Name	Developer	URL	Strengths	Limitations	Suggestions
Activity Pattern Blocks	Jacobo Bulaevsky	forum.swarthmore.edu/ sum95/suzanne/ active.html	Clear, simple design. Exercise to teach the vocabulary of polygons. Detailed explanation for using the pattern blocks.	Poor navigation.	Install navigation icons.
Math Baseball	Funbrain Company	www.funbrain.com/mat h/ index.html	Detailed explanation of the game rules.	Long load times. Text & graphics only.	Add animation & sound.
The Abacus: The Art of Calculating with Beads	Luis Fernandes	www.ee.ryerson.ca/~elf/ abacus	Informative, interactive site. Intuitive interface: student uses an abacus by clicking on its beads. Available in 4 foreign languages.	Tiny abacus. Poor navigation. Low readability due to small font size.	Enlarge the abacus. Increase font size. Add sound effects when user clicks on a bead.
Lemonade Stands	Jason Mayans	www.littlejason.com/ lemonade/index.html	Interesting interactive simulation program. Simple design. Friendly user interface. Motivation by viewing high scores of previous users.	Long time to load. No navigation icons.	Use additional multimedia. Award prizes to enhance motivation.
Base Ten Count	Education by Design Inc.	www.edbydesign.com/ btcount.html	Interactive multimedia instruction. A helpful guide to the game. Simple game design.	Small images & text. Long load times. Inadequate sound effects.	Develop an avatar to guide users.

A comparison of the entries with those in the first table highlights the relative independence of illustrious sites and packages. In particular, exemplary software is often available at Websites of modest means. The converse may also occur, where a site offers a wealth of resources, but does not excel in any particular direction. The diversity of approaches and flair in implementation underscores the utility of benchmarking vanguard sites.

As indicated in the charts, the portfolio of Websites and programs displayed a number of progressive features. Even so, each had its limitations and offered room for improvement.

One implication is the need for a Website which incorporates the best features of extant examples while avoiding their drawbacks. The portal would take full advantage of digital capabilities as they mature.

For this task, a prime consideration lies in the potential for a digital technology to convey content in a compelling way. On the other hand, a technique which is too novel or unstable can be cumbersome for both the developer and user. In that case, it would be better to wait for the maturation of the technology before incorporating it into a site addressed to all levels of visitors - both novices and experts in the use of online tools.

For these reasons, the design of a site has to strike a balance between innovation and the stability of the candidate technologies. The applications described below illustrate the quest for innovation while taking account of the merits of technological maturity.

Progressive Applications

An online forum for mathematics education is found at WebMath, a resource located at *www.webmath.org*. The Website offers content in both English and Korean. Certain materials are available in both languages, while the majority of the content is in one or the other language.

The Website contains examples of multimedia software. At the turn of the decade, one item available at the site was the Probability Concepts module, an interactive animation to teach the basics of probability theory and its applications. Another piece, the Fractal Patterns program, was designed to teach the geometry of chaotic processes. To enhance user interest, the material was presented in the form of a solitary game.

A third program taught spatial reasoning to high school students using virtual reality techniques. A field study of the software at two high schools verified the utility of the software for learning about spatial geometry.

As with any construct, the programs at WebMath had their advantages and limitations. The package at the site reflected early efforts in online education and was slated to give way to superior content over the years.

Progress in digital techniques continues to drive advances in Web-based education. As a case in point, the use of streaming media to convey video presentations was a primary concern for leading universities at the dawn of the millennium.

In the late 1990s, vanguard institutions gathered together to form an educational consortium known as Internet 2. The mission of the alliance was to pursue a diverse collection of pedagogical applications in cyberspace. The projects ranged from music lessons on the Net to mobile collaboration through wireless devices.

A sampling of future directions for the Web is highlighted in Table C.3. In the decades ahead, these capabilities should find their way into products at all levels, from preschool edutainment to professional training. The educational systems will build on, and contribute to, the gamut of products in other spheres such as work and play.

Table C.3. Some promising directions for Web-based education.

Capability	Strengths	Limitations	Suggestions
Multiple users in interaction.	Learning from other users. Socializing and communal support.	Limited graphics and bandwidth make interactions cumbersome and slow.	Problems will decline with advancing network capabilities.
Representation of users by avatars.	Personalization of cyberspace. An avatar can take over simple behaviors when owner is offline.	Easy to hide behind a mask and engage in disruptive behavior.	Require greater authentication.
Engagement through edutainment, including games.	Learning is more compelling and memorable.	Not all instruction is amenable to a gaming format.	Develop new forms of edutainment.
Data mining and artificial life.	Smart tutors to guide students. Evolutionary software to challenge users.	Difficult to produce versatile intelligence.	Adapt additional concepts from neurology, biology, psychology, etc.
Web access on mobile phones.	Education anytime, anywhere.	Small screens.	Extensible and/or flexible screen. Holographic projections in future devices.

Summary

Cyberspace offers a pliable milieu for the wealth of information being digitized all over the globe. The ascent of multimedia channels on the Net has led to a popular vehicle for presenting content in a compelling way. The active role of the user in navigating a virtual space and the instant response of the system provide an immersive experience for solitary exploration as well as group interaction.

A prime direction for the future lies in autonomous learning software. The maturation of machine learning allows for smart agents which can tailor a presentation not only to the general level of expertise for a particular student, but also to his or her expanding scope of knowledge. The adaptive features may be implemented through techniques such as case based reasoning, neural networks, and induction.

A digital aide may be deployed as the kernel of an adept system for multimedia presentations. A conceptual framework for such intelligent systems has been available since the 1990s.[52] Further, the architecture for intelligent presentations has been adapted to software agents and their embodiment as graphic objects.[53]

At various centers of research and development around the world, efforts are under way to harness knowledge based schemes for educational systems. The techniques behind the pedagogical projects are drawing on, and providing inspiration for, other types of applications. Examples of generic capabilities include the retrieval of video files based on semantic content and the coordination of distributed sites to support online meetings among remote participants.

In future, personal agents will be on call around the clock to provide learning on demand. Smart agents armed with adaptive techniques will be able to mold a presentation in tune with the background of the user as well as her needs of the moment.

Appendix D

Discovering Knowledge in Cyberland

The automated approach to knowledge discovery, also known as data mining, came of age in the 1990s. The methods of knowledge mining now serve as the bedrock for a new generation of smart software. The technology represents an indispensable toolkit for analysis in business, engineering, science, and government.

A competent program should possess greater functionality than merely fetch data or broadcast basic facts. Rather, an intelligent agent should be able to perform routine tasks autonomously, glean new knowledge from disparate databases, and improve its own performance through experience.

Where is the field of knowledge mining headed over the coming years? The paths of growth lie in greater intelligence as well as the embodiment of adaptive schemes within animated agents. Digital aides have already begun to acquire personalities and accompany surfers as they wander through the virtual worlds of the Internet.

An introduction to knowledge mining was presented in Chapter 2. This appendix examines some basic issues behind the design of nimble agents, offers a general architecture, and presents case studies in design and forecasting.

Flavors of Data Mining

In recent years, interest in data mining has percolated across the panoply of human endeavors. The ascendance of the technology stems mainly from the efficacy of autolearning tools in comparison to traditional schemes in fields ranging from business and economics to medicine, engineering, and entertainment.

Data mining – comprising the entire bag of tools from machine learning, statistics, and visualization – has had a long lineage. The roots of visualization schemes might be traced to the dawn of mankind, when our ancestors first etched figures on the walls of a cave or scratched maps in the sand with broken twigs.

In a sense, the field of statistics emerged with the counting of prey or the accounting of tools arrayed against a wall. Only in the past century, however, has statistics blossomed into a formal discipline.

Machine learning refers to techniques for enhancing the performance of a system over time. In the simplest conception, a single program may be regarded as a learning machine if its ability improves with an expansion of its attendant database. For instance, forecasts of the chance of snow in Oslo on Christmas Day are likely to improve as the number of observations increases, even if the predictive procedure remains unchanged. A rise in performance based on a static procedure but dynamic database might be classified as zeroth-order learning. This category includes many traditional algorithms which are not classified as machine learning; but it also encompasses a number of adaptive schemes such as induction or case based reasoning.

The next level of learning involves an improvement in performance even with a static input: the procedure evolves despite its reliance on a frozen database. This type of improvement might be called first-order learning. We could consider a genetic algorithm to be an exemplar of this category, since its performance evolves over time. On the other hand, the performance of the system tends to increase at first, but gradually levels off toward an asymptote or limiting value.

The neural network – in its diverse forms – represents an entire class of techniques which shares some traits with genetic algorithms. Both types of schemes are based on biological metaphors: the neural net on the structure of a single brain and the genetic algorithm on the evolution of chromosomes in a fluid population. The neural network, like the genetic algorithm, tends to enhance its performance during an initial transient stage, then settle toward an asymptote.

Another group of techniques relates to second-order learning: a type of procedure to identify which of several elementary schemes is most suited for addressing a particular task. In a sense, a second-order algorithm learns how to learn, since it strives to identify the best learning method for each problem or case.

Yet other types of algorithms are possible. For instance, one approach is to use a genetic algorithm to optimize the weights used to rank neighbors during case based reasoning. This nested methodology could be regarded as a first-order technique; or since it involves a synergistic mixture of first-order techniques, a label such as 1.5-order learning might be more appropriate. No doubt the future will throw up higher-order models with even greater capacity to adapt and generalize.

Smart Agents

An *agent* is an autonomous system capable of making decisions on behalf of another entity.[54] The purpose of the activity is to support some goal of a user, or another agent whose ultimate objective is the fulfillment of human needs.

The mental state of an agent refers to the collective condition of internal modules such as capabilities, obligations, beliefs, and decisions.[55] The activities of agents are controlled by scripts or itineraries, including operations for communicating with other entities.

A number of desirable attributes for agents may be identified. Two such behavioral principles are competence and trust.[56] *Competence* refers to learning capability: the enhancement of performance with accumulating experience. *Trust* is a projective rather than an inherent attribute: it refers to the comfort level of the user which evolves over time, along with his mental model of the agent's competencies and idiosyncrasies.

Additional desiderata for autonomous agents lie in goal orientation, charity, balance, and integration.[57] A *goal-oriented* agent is one that responds to what a user needs, then autonomously determines how to achieve the result. An agent is *charitable* when it tends to forgive mistakes: it regards the user's stated request as a clue to the desired result rather than a literal and complete specification. A *balanced* aide is one that weighs the cost and potential mistakes of seeking information autonomously against the nuisance of pestering the user for clarification. An *integrated* agent is one which presents a uniform interface to the user while providing a wide range of services, from sending email to negotiating an agreement.

Another important trait for an agent lies in security. *Security* may be further categorized into safety and privacy. *Safety* refers to the use of safeguards to prevent or limit undesirable side effects. For instance, an agent should not cavalierly delete a unique but important document merely to free disk space and thereby improve system responsiveness. The second aspect of security lies in privacy. To maintain *privacy*, an agent must avoid divulging sensitive facts from internal storage or acquiring confidential information from external sources without proper authorization.

Agents on Networks

One way to classify agents is in terms of mobility. A *sedentary* agent resides permanently on a particular machine and handles local tasks, as exemplified by a user-friendly interface to a complex application package.[58] On the other hand, a *mobile* agent travels across a network to pursue high-intensity tasks such as a protracted negotiation.[59]

An intelligent agent is a flexible program characterized by adaptability and autonomy.[60] The more a user comes to depend on a particular agent, the greater is the need for the program to adapt to his habits and needs.[61]

Against the backdrop of an open network, security is a paramount concern for both agents and servers.[62] Agents must be protected against accidental damage or deliberate attempts to extract sealed information. In a similar way, servers must be made secure against deliberate intrusions or inadvertent mishaps due to errant visitors from the network.

To work in a distributed environment, an agent must be able to accommodate a diverse set of formats for knowledge representation and database management.[63] An adept aide has to recognize common standards such as the Knowledge Query and Manipulation Language (KQML).[64] In addition, the ability to wander readily across a network points toward an implementation platform such as Java: a language characterized by compactness, robustness, speed, security, and object-orientation.[65]

The preceding topics represent basic issues in the design and implementation of agents on an electronic network. The general architecture presented in the next section reflects the preceding concerns as well as other salient issues in the design of intelligent systems.[66]

Design on the Web

To illustrate the deployment of adroit agents in a network environment, we turn to a case study from the field of engineering. The software employs the technique of case based reasoning (CBR) as the kernel of a distributed system to support collaborative design.

The World Wide Design Lab is a flexible platform which stores each design or case at a single site among participating organizations in the U.S. and Europe.[67] To minimize data transmission across the Internet, the case registry on a central server stores only the key features needed to identify an archived example. For instance, the size of an engine for a particular truck might be stored on the server, but not the type of steering wheel. When the repository receives a request for a precedent design from a user, the server consults the case registry to identify the desired item, then asks the host computer of the latter record to transmit all pertinent data directly to the requesting computer. In this way, traffic on the Internet is kept to a small number which is independent of the numerosity of participating locations or the number of records in the case base at any particular site.

Intelligent Multimedia

The need for smart systems is underscored by the rapid accumulation of content on the Net. In addition to the sheer volume of material, the knowledge is available in diverse formats ranging from text and audio to video and virtual reality.

Moreover, the same material may be used for different purposes. For instance, a virtual model of an airplane might be molded during the design of the vehicle, but later used by a safety instructor to point out the locations of emergency exits.

An adaptive agent can serve as a friendly interface to any informatic system. To illustrate, a smart system for design knowledge can automate tasks such as the following.

- Identification of precedent cases.
- Retrieval of pertinent information for a particular case.

● Integration of materials for presentation to the user.
● Adaptation of materials based on the observed level of user expertise.

A versatile system should provide an integrated platform which understands high-level commands and tailors a presentation to the current needs of the user.

A simple configuration for an intelligent multimedia system is shown in Figure D.1. The external interface is regulated by a knowledge based module which manages each session according to the behavior of the user as well as the contents of the multimedia database.

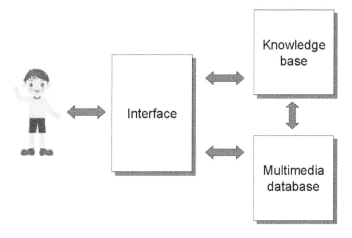

Figure D.1. General schematic for a smart multimedia system.

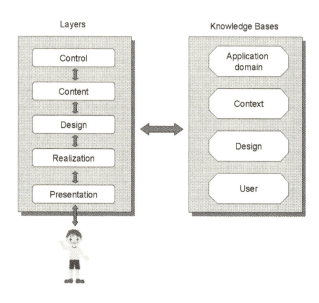

Figure D.2. Reference model for IMMPS.

A general model for an intelligent multimedia presentation system (IMMPS) is given in Figure D.2. The layered architecture comprises five levels ranging from presentation to control. The layers are coordinated by knowledge bases relating to the profile of the user and the design of the presentation; other components include the historical context behind the session plus a model of the application domain.[68]

The IMMPS framework is a convenient scheme for creating a modular interface. It has been utilized, for instance, in crafting the functionality of the Personalized Plan-based Presenter: an agent which utilizes animated avatars to present requested information.[69] For instance, the system employs a cartoon figure which wields a wand in one hand to point out a component in a technical diagram, while a second wand in the other hand refers to the corresponding text in a different window on the user's monitor.

System architecture. An intelligent agent must be able to work in a distributed environment characterized by diverse hardware platforms, database structures, and application packages. More generally, an adaptive agent has to function robustly in a heterogeneous network and interact effectively with other programs.

Figure D.3 presents the block structure of a digital agent. The structure begins with a component to uniquely identify the entity, followed by modules for its planned schedule and internal condition. The next segment specifies the behaviors available to the agent, while the last module is a temporary region for use as a scratchpad.

Agent Identification	*Agenda*	*Status*	*Behavior*	*Working Memory*

Figure D.3. Block structure for defining an agent. The behaviors pertain to autonomous actions, message handling, and other activities.

Figure D.4 identifies two types of agents: immortals which persist indefinitely, and mortals which expire at the end of their respective missions. Zeus is the supervisory agent on the application server, and Athena the gatekeeper for the database server. Odysseus is a mobile agent which roams across the network to procure information as needed. Hermes, on the other hand, is a local courier which conveys routine messages on the intranet. Helen is the mediating agent which provides a friendly interface between the user and the rest of the system.

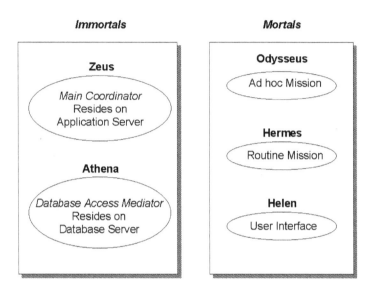

Figure D.4. Dramatis personae of agent types in a global network.

The family of programs can be used to implement a society of collaborating agents across a network. Since the functionality is generic, the architecture and agent profiles may be cloned for diverse domains such as education, entertainment, marketing, or planning.

Multistrategy learning. As explained in Chapter 2, a neural network (NN) offers many advantages such as robustness and graceful degradation.[70] However, most neural nets suffer from various limitations such as the need for long learning times. A second drawback lies in the implicit nature of the acquired knowledge, which is generally difficult for a human to decipher.[71] This disadvantage is reflected in the ability to perform well – such as in predicting a stock market – without yielding an explicit explanation of the causative factors behind the analysis.[72]

Another versatile technique is found in case based reasoning. A key advantage of case based reasoning lies in the ability to work with data in their original format. Often the methodology is effective even when applied to an incomplete or partially faulty database. One drawback, however, lies in the tendency of conventional CBR tools to identify similarities based on superficial rather than substantive features of two cases. However, this is a liability applicable to the entire gamut of learning tools.

Induction refers to the generation of rules or the classification of objects into decision trees. The scheme generates new knowledge in the explicit form of rules or trees.[73] However, the procedure can be cumbersome to use and has not been deployed as widely as it deserves.

Second-order learning is a multistrategy approach to predictive decision making. For this method, the first stage of the integrated architecture involves a basic set of learning models. The outputs from these models enter a second stage. The latter then determines which of the values from the initial stage to use for each instance of the problem.[74] The general methodology is depicted in Figure D.5, where the output from each module is labeled as a candidate forecast.

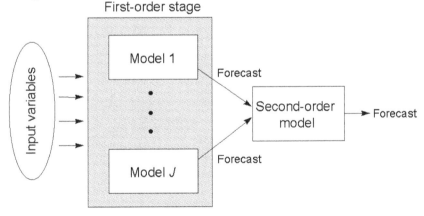

Figure D.5. Schematic of the second-order learning architecture in the context of a predictive application.

At the secondary stage, a suitable method from machine learning can be used to select among the outputs from the elementary modules. The basic techniques for first-order learning might take the form of, say, CBR and a neural network.

Meanwhile, induction could be used as the second-order procedure. With this choice, induction serves as a metalevel predictor to determine the conditions under which CBR outperforms the neural network, or vice versa. Then the forecast from the superior method can be selected on a case-by-case basis to determine the output of the overall system.

Case Study in Prediction

The integrated approach to knowledge mining may be illustrated through a case study in the prediction of overall capacity utilization among all industries. In addition to the target variable in the form of total utilization (TOT), three other input factors were employed in the application: capacity utilization for the manufacturing (MFG), mining (MNG), and utility (UTI) sectors.

The database consisted of monthly observations of the four variables from January 1967 to April 1997, as indicated in Table D.1. The test phase ran from January 1985 to April 1997.

Table D.1. List of input variables. Data were monthly observations from January 1967 to April 1997.

Label	Name	Description
TOT	Total industry	Total capacity utilization among all industries
MFG	Manufacturing	Capacity utilization for manufacturing sector
MNG	Mining	Capacity utilization for mining sector
UTI	Utilities	Capacity utilization for utilities

A variety of adaptive schemes was hitched to the task of predicting the target variable. The first procedure was a case based reasoning model using the 4 available variables in conjunction with 5 precedent cases. This model was labeled CBR5. The mean absolute percent error (MAPE) for the forecasts was approximately 0.34 percent.

The second scheme involved CBR using 4 inputs and 20 neighbors. For this model, tagged as CBR20, the MAPE was 0.49 percent.

The third algorithm was a neural network model with 4 input nodes, 4 hidden nodes, and 1 output node. The MAPE for this model was 0.41 percent.

Finally, an inductive procedure based on the ID3 algorithm was examined. Since the procedure yields a classification corresponding to a discrete set of outcomes, only a binary forecast was generated. More precisely, the prediction involved a comparison of the current value $x(t)$ of the target variable at time t against that of the forecast $f(t+1)$ for the subsequent period. If $f(t+1) \geq x(t)$, then the prediction was labeled *up*; otherwise it was labeled *down*.

The induction algorithm produced a decision tree which is portrayed in Figure D.6. The interpretation of the hierarchy may be illustrated by a traversal down the branch on the right side at each junction, starting with the root node at the top. For this chain of branches, the sequence of decisions and the final outcome is equivalent to the following rule.

IF	the value of TOT at time t is *up* compared to that at the previous period $t - 1$,
AND	MFG at t is *up* compared to $t - 1$,
AND	UTI at t is *up* compared to $t - 1$,
AND	MNG at t is *up* compared to $t - 1$:
THEN	TOT at $t + 1$ will be *up* with probability 0.25, and *down* with probability 0.75.

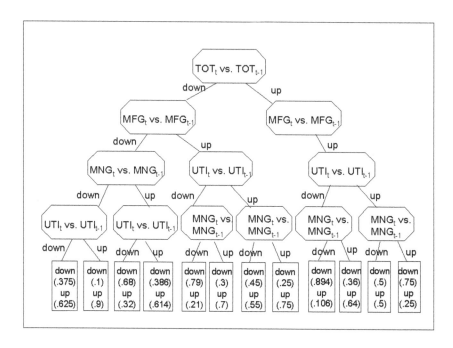

Figure D.6. Induction tree resulting from the ID3 algorithm.

Given the binary forecasts from the induction procedure, the elementary schemes were compared using the yardstick of *hit rate*: the proportion of correct forecasts. According to this measure, each of the CBR and NN techniques outperformed the induction algorithm.

Among the elementary methods, CBR20 and NN yielded the best hit rates. For this reason, the latter two models were selected as the first stage of the integrated architecture. The second stage relied on the ID3 procedure, while employing the input data and outputs from the first stage of the architecture.

For the integrated learning scheme, the dataset was partitioned into three parts. The first portion, Segment A, covered the period from January 1967 to December 1975. This was followed by Segment B from

January 1976 to December 1984. The remainder of the data stream was marked as Segment C.

For the compound architecture, the inductive scheme in the metalevel module was trained on the data and results associated with Segment B of the data set. The goal of the second stage was to discern whether the output from CBR20 would be more accurate than that from NN, or vice versa. Finally, all five architectures were tested using Segment C of the data set.

The models were compared against the metric of hit rate. The results in Table D.2 indicate that the basic induction module performed the worst, while the second-order architecture bested the others.

Table D.2. Comparison of predictive methods.

Model	Hit Rate
CBR (5 neighbors)	0.7891
CBR (20 neighbors)	0.8367
Neural Network	0.7915
Induction	0.7542
Second-order Learning	0.8824

It is interesting to note the superiority of the integrated model, even though it employed the inductive procedure which had fared the worst among the elementary techniques. The outcome was indicative of synergism at work: inferior components, when assembled in a constructive way, can yield superior performance.

Summary

The rapid expansion of cyberspace and the accelerating pace of transactions highlight the need for clever agents to support human users. To this end, learning agents may be deployed to automate routine tasks, glean useful knowledge, and enhance system performance.

Each approach in the field of machine learning has its pluses and minuses. To circumvent the limitations, a clutch of elementary methods can be integrated into hybrid approaches such as second-order learning.

The future holds many possibilities, including the incorporation of emergent concepts and tools from the field of artificial life. The road ahead will lead to a lively ecosystem of agents to enrich the human experience in all areas of work, play and study.

Appendix E

Exercises

A. Problems on the Web

1: This exercise involves a comparative evaluation of Websites on the electronic highway. A number of sources on the Internet offer "hot lists", or links to innovative Web applications. For instance, you could access the Yahoo portal at the following location:

http://www.yahoo.com

At the site, you can use the search facility by entering the keywords "top Web sites". The search engine should return a list of sites Which offer "hot lists". Among the sites identified, you are to select an interesting entry and proceed to it. Then follow the links from the latter site (which offers a collection of hot lists) to two target sites which seem appealing. Your next tasks are as follows.

a. For each site, explain the reasons for your selection.
b. Describe the key features of each site.

c. What are the relative strengths and weaknesses of the two sites?

d. For each site, what are your recommendations for improvement and/or suggestions regarding future directions?

Your work will be evaluated according to the following criteria.

1) Functionality, relating to the effectiveness of your argument.
   ● How well are the key issues identified and expressed?
   ● What data—either documented or estimated—are used to support your arguments?
2) Originality, in terms of the freshness and creativity of your analysis plus synthesis of ideas.
3) Clarity, pertaining to the simplicity of your exposition.

Your assignment will be presented in class and your slides or viewgraphs submitted for grading as well. The delivery of your presentation and your viewgraphs will receive equal weighting in your grade. The only written record required for this assignment is the set of viewgraphs you prepare for your presentation.

2:   Since the mid-1990s, Microsoft Corp. has been embracing cyberspace with great zeal. Today, the corporate Website is one of the most popular destinations for electronic voyagers:

//www.microsoft.com

Over the years, Microsoft has launched numerous services and programs on the Net, ranging from an online travel agent to a game portal. Your task is to select one of the electronic services available from the Microsoft federation. Then do the following.

a. Describe the service.
b. Analyze the pros and cons of the site, including its "business model": that is, how it is designed to earn money in order to continue to provide services.
c. Recommend ways in which to improve the *Website*, the *service*, and the *business model*.
d. Discuss the strengths and limitations of your suggestions from Step (c) above.

3: You are to perform a comparative evaluation of educational sites in cyberspace. After reviewing a variety of educational sites on the Internet, create your own "hot list" of the top 3 sites. Analyze each site as outlined in Parts (a) through (d) of Exercise A2 above.
Hint. For this and other exercises, you may wish to draw on the resources at About.com. The portal is located at: about.com

4: This exercise is intended to provide you with practice in developing Web-based material without writing HTML code. In particular, you will create a homepage for yourself.

1) Using a Web browser, access the homepages of several people in different countries. You will find such Websites at all sorts of universities or other institutions. Another source of homepages is available at this URL:

www.geocities.com

a. Select 3 of the most innovative homepages that you encounter.

b. Identify the strengths and limitations of each of these sites.

c. Present suggestions for improving each site.

2) For this task, you first need to deploy the Communicator package from Netscape. You can download the software by accessing the following site from your browser:

home.netscape.com

Then follow the instructions at the Website in order to download the installation software and set up the Communicator system on your computer. After starting the Communicator program, proceed with the mouse to the toolbar at the top of the window. Then select the Composer option from the Communicator menu. Within Composer, type a few words. You will note that the software is intuitive to use, and works much like a word processor such as Microsoft Word. From Composer, you can also access external Websites, modify the downloaded pages, and save those pages to your own hard disk. To this end, you can select the "Open Page" option from the File menu. Then type in a URL such as:

ibm.com

in order to access the site for IBM from Composer.

3) Finally, create a homepage for yourself. In addition to crafting original material, it is possible to borrow certain

items such as buttons or other objects available on the Net. From external Websites, you may copy any material which is not proprietary or copyrighted. Of course, whenever you use such content, you should give proper credit where it is due.

5:     A "think tank" is research center which explores vanguard ideas. In the field of digital media, one of the most innovative centers is found at the MIT Media Lab:

www.media.mit.edu

At this site, you will find a number of research projects ranging from personalized newspapers to wearable computers.

Your first task is to examine several projects and their associated technologies. Then perform the following analysis.

a. Describe the project and the technologies involved.
b. Identify potential changes in lifestyle 20 years from now as a result of these technologies.
c. Generate ideas for 5 novel products (goods or services) based on these technologies.
d. Evaluate your ideas from Part (c) above: strengths, limitations, and suggestions.

6:     A popular set of tools for developing multimedia products is available from Macromedia Inc. Take a look at the following site:

www.macromedia.com

Your task is to select two software *applications* which have been developed using tools from Macromedia.

a. Describe each system or application package.

b. Evaluate each system in terms of its relative strengths and limitations.

c. Provide suggestions for improvement based on your evaluation.

7:   As indicated above, a variety of tools for developing multimedia products is on offer at Macromedia Inc. The firm provides utilities for developing multimedia products, such as the Authorware package for creating instructional software. You are to select one of these *tools* – other than Flash or Dreamweaver – and analyze it.

a. Describe the tool: What it is, why it's useful, and so on.

b. Evaluate the product in terms of its strengths and limitations.

c. Provide suggestions for improvement based on your evaluation.

d. Describe how the tool might be helpful in implementing your term project.

8:   In the realm of commercial products, some of the leading-edge applications of multimedia capabilities are found in digital entertainment. From the Net, you are to select two multimedia games in the "adventure" category.

a. Briefly describe each game.

b. Identify the relative advantages and limitations of the games.

c. Recommend ways in which additional capabilities can be employed to further enhance each product.

d. Explain the strengths and limitations of your recommendations above.

A good place to start your search for products is the following site: gamespot.com.

9:     Select two multimedia games in the "puzzle" category which are available on the Internet.

a. Briefly describe each game.
b. Identify the relative advantages and limitations of the games.
c. Recommend ways in which additional capabilities can be employed to further enhance each product.
d. Explain the strengths and limitations of your recommendations above.

A good place to start your search for products is the portal at Yahoo: games.yahoo.com.

10:     Select two online gaming services offering products for multiple players.

a. Briefly describe each service, including revenue sources and examples of games that are offered (show some screen shots or video clips from demos).
b. Identify the relative advantages and limitations of each service.
c. Recommend ways in which additional capabilities can be employed to further enhance each service or product.
d. Explain the strengths and limitations of your recommendations above.

11:     The Knowledge Media Institute at the Open University in
        England is a progressive center for multimedia and online
        systems. The homepage for KMI identifies a number of
        categories for research projects:

                            kmi.open.ac.uk

        You are to first select one category which appeals to you. Next,
        follow a link to some interesting project. Finally, consider the
        questions below.

        a. Briefly describe the system. You should include some screen
           shots or video clips of demos if software is available online;
           otherwise you will have to rely solely on the documentation
           provided at the site.
        b. Describe the advantages and limitations of the system.
        c. Recommend ways in which additional multimedia
           capabilities can be employed to further enhance the system.
        d. Explain the strengths and limitations of your
           recommendations above.

12:     Another interesting site is maintained by the School of
        Cognitive and Computing Sciences (COGS) at the University
        of Sussex in England. The homepage for COGS identifies a
        number of interesting projects.

                    www.cogs.susx.ac.uk/lab/adapt/index.html

        You are to select one project at COGS which interests you.
        Then answer the types of questions in the preceding exercise.

B. Hands-on Lessons with Flash

The exercises in this section will provide you with the basic skills needed to create some interesting animations. Your first task is to study the appropriate lesson. Next, you are to construct - where possible - a simple but original piece of work which demonstrates your mastery of the techniques in the lesson.

Finally, you are to present your work and explain the procedure you employed to produce your handiwork. Your presentation should cover the following topics.

a. Explanation of key points in the lesson.
b. Demonstration of your own handicraft.
c. Procedure for creating your piece in Part (b) above.
d. Analysis in terms of strengths, limitations and suggestions for improvement relating to:
> 1) The interactive lesson which you summarized in Part (a) above.
> 2) Your handiwork presented in Part (b) above.

The preceding outline should be followed in presenting your report after performing each of the drills specified below.

1:     You are to download a copy of the Flash software. To obtain the *trial version* of the program, you need to take the following steps.

● Using your browser such as Netscape Navigator, access the following Website.

http://macromedia.com/software/downloads/

- Follow the links to the software that you need. In particular, to obtain a copy of the Flash program, click on your mouse for the appropriate link(s) indicated at the site. At the Macromedia site, you may have to answer some questions before downloading the software.

- (Double) click on the item you selected in the preceding step. This will start the process of copying the program onto your own PC. If you are asked any questions which you are uncertain about, it is simplest to answer "Yes". You should keep track of where the program is being downloaded onto your PC; it will likely be a folder on your "C" disk drive.

- At this point, you should have a copy of the *setup* program for the actual software that you need. Locate the setup program on your hard disk, then double click on it to start the installation process. You should follow the suggestions provided by the installation software, such as re-starting your computer if directed to do so.

2:   The package that you installed in Exercise B1 above includes the trial version of the software as well as supplementary materials, including an electronic manual entitled *Using Flash*. You should print this manual to obtain a hard copy; an alternative is to procure a nicely formatted version of the document, which you can download from *macromedia.com*. As explained near the front of the manual, the lessons for the Flash utility can be accessed from the Help menu of the software tool. You are to perform Lessons 1 through 4. Then prepare a presentation as indicated in topics (a) through (d) above.

3:      Your task is to perform the remaining Lessons in the Help section of the Flash program.

4:      Do the drills in Chapter 1 of the manual *Using Flash*. Then prepare a report as indicated in topics (a) through (d) above.

5:      Study Chapter 2 of the manual.

6:      Study Chapter 3 of the manual.

7:      Study Chapter 4 of the manual.

8:      Study Chapter 5 of the manual.

9:      Study Chapters 6 and 7 of the manual.

10:     Study the remaining sections of the manual at the rate of two chapters per day.

C. Hands-on Lessons with Dreamweaver

The exercises in this section will provide you with the basic skills needed to create an interesting *Website*. Your first task is to study the appropriate lesson. Next, you are to construct - where possible - a simple but original piece of work which demonstrates your mastery of the techniques in the lesson.

Finally, you are to present your work and explain the procedure you employed to produce your handiwork. Your presentation should over the following items.

a. Explanation of key points in the lesson.

b. Demonstration of your own handicraft.

c. Procedure for creating your piece in Part (b) above.

d. Analysis in terms of strengths, limitations and suggestions for improvement relating to:

    1) The interactive lesson which you summarized in Part (a) above.

    2) Your handiwork presented in Part (b) above.

The preceding outline should be followed in preparing your report after performing each of the drills specified below.

1:     Your first task is to download a copy of the Dreamweaver software. To obtain the *trial version* of the software, you need to take the following steps.

- Using your browser such as Netscape Navigator, access the following Web site.

  http://macromedia.com

- Follow the links to the software that you need. In particular, to obtain a copy of the Dreamweaver program, click on your mouse for the appropriate link(s) indicated at the site. At the Macromedia site, you may have to answer some questions before downloading the software.

- (Double) click on the item you selected in the preceding step. This will start the process of copying the program onto your own PC. If you are asked any questions which you are uncertain about, it is simplest to answer "Yes". You should keep track of where the program is being downloaded onto your PC; it will likely be a folder in your "C" disk drive.

● At this point, you should have a copy of the *setup* program for the actual software that you need. Locate the setup program on your hard disk, then double click on it to start the installation process. You should follow the suggestions provided by the installation software, such as re-starting your computer if directed to do so.

2:    The package that you installed in Exercise C1 above includes the trial version of the software as well as supplementary materials, including an electronic manual entitled *Using Dreamweaver*. You should print this manual to obtain a hard copy; an alternative is to download a nicely formatted copy of the document from the *macromedia.com* site.

As explained near the front of the manual, an overview of the Dreamweaver package can be accessed from the Help menu of the software tool. You are to follow the Guided Tour from the Help menu of Dreamweaver. Then prepare a presentation as indicated in Items (a) through (d) of the report format specified above.

3:    Study the first half of the Tutorial in Chapter 1 of the manual *Using Dreamweaver*. Then prepare a presentation as indicated in Items (a) through (d) of the report format specified above.

4:    Study the second half of the Tutorial in Chapter 1 of the manual *Using Dreamweaver*. Then prepare a presentation as indicated in Items (a) through (d) of the report format specified above.

5:    Study Chapter 2 of the manual.

6:        Study Chapter 3 of the manual.

7:        Study Chapter 4 of the manual.

8:        Study Chapter 5 of the manual.

9:        Study Chapters 6 and 7 of the manual.

10:       Study the remaining sections of the manual at the rate of two
          chapters per day.

D. Group Exercises

1:        **Breakout Session.** In this exercise, you will form teams and
          design an informatic strategy for a global firm. Your first step
          is to select an interesting industry, be it telecommunications,
          banking, automobiles, travel, leisure, biotechnology, and so
          on. For your industry of choice, identify the leading firm of
          world-class stature. While conducting this exercise, you may
          wish to review Chapters 2 and 5, among others.
          Your discussion should cover the following topics.

          ● Identification of emerging digital technologies.
          ● Ways in which the technologies can transform
            organizational structures and business processes within
            the firm you selected.
          ● Ways in which the technologies can be employed to
            support interactions with external stakeholders:
            customers, suppliers, collaborators, government
            agencies, and so on.
          ● Recommendations and anticipated benefits for your
            selected firm.

Before you begin your discussion, you should elect the following officers for your group: *timekeeper, scribe* (to record ideas), and *spokesperson* (to present the results).

2.   **Group Collaboration.** Electronic conferencing is a popular mode of collaboration in many fields, ranging from education to product design and project management. The purpose of this exercise is to provide you with direct practice in using the Internet to collaborate with your classmates and resolve meaningful queries. The procedure is as follows.

After reviewing the topics discussed in class and/or the readings, you are to identify a question which other people might find interesting. An example of an elementary query is, "What is the best estimate of the amount of online sales in the U.S. last year?" On the other hand, a more sophisticated question is "How will the Internet affect buying patterns for various product categories, 5 years from now?"

a. You are to post your question on the class Website, as well as discuss it with your friends through email, cyberchat, and/or in person.

Note. Any document you submit or forward to any other participant should contain the following identifiers: your name, ID number, and email address.

b. You are to examine the questions posted by two other classmates. Next you should provide electronic references which might be useful for them, as well as forward a copy of the pertinent document(s). (When you "forward" the document from a Web browser such as Netscape Navigator, the document's address will be appended automatically.)

c. After considering the influx of messages from Step (b) above in response to your own question from Step (a), you are to compose a thoughtful summary.

d. You should document the results of Steps (b) and (c) above, then post it on the Website for the course.

The evaluation of your work will be based on a variety of criteria. In particular, you should strive for functionality (how thoughtful or meaningful is your contribution), originality (how creative), simplicity (how clear), and efficiency (how concise, subject to attaining the functionality).

E. Miniproject 1

This *miniproject* involves the investigation of different forms of edutainment. In particular, the task will offer an opportunity for you to wield a variety of concepts and techniques presented in the text. The miniproject will be an individual endeavor which exercises your imagination, creativity, and resourcefulness.

Comic strips have been used as a user-friendly format to teach serious subjects ranging from history to mathematics. Such texts are available in a variety of languages, from English and Swedish to Korean and Japanese. For this exercise, you will analyze several examples of educational comics and create a simple Web-based product of your own.

a.   Identify a variety of comic strips of the pedagogical genre. The comics may be in hardcopy format, such as a paper book, or softcopy, such as a digital animation. Analyze each of these samples in terms of (i) a brief description, (ii) evaluation of strengths and limitations, and (iii) suggestions for improvement.

b.   Develop an outline for implementing your own Web-based comics. Moreover, you should identify the pertinent Web-based tool(s) for each module.

c.   Create an improved, Web-based version of one of the comic strips in some field, such as algebra, economics, or art. Your demo should be brief but captivating; a user should be able to get through the material in about 5 to 10 minutes.

Your report should be in the form of a *demo* of your handicraft plus *slides* or *viewgraphs*: figures, tables, images, and brief passages of text. Your presentation - including a demo of your system - should be packed with interesting facts and ideas, but well rehearsed for delivery within a few minutes.

Grading. The project represents an opportunity to demonstrate your understanding of the concepts covered in lectures. In general, your grade will be based on your creative application of the ideas and tools discussed in class. Your report will be evaluated along the following criteria.

- *Functionality:* effectiveness of your analysis and your recommendations.
- *Originality:* novelty of your approach to analysis as well as creativity in the synthesis of your multimedia piece.
- *Simplicity:* conceptual elegance of your approach and clarity of your report.
- *Efficiency:* minimal use of resources in your handiwork and compactness of your report, consistent with the attainment of your objectives.

Miniproject 2

This miniproject involves an analysis of Websites relating to educational or gaming software. You should first select a category such as virtual universities, commercial training institutes, or online gaming services. Next you are to identify the best sites in the chosen category, then evaluate the hosting organizations and the programs they offer.

Your report should include the following sections.

A. Summary.
B. Typology: Classification of Different Types of Websites.
C. Case Studies.
    1. Top Web *Site* in Each Category in Step B above.
    2. Top *Program* in Each Category.
D. Conceptual Design for a Novel Website

The case studies in Part C above should include a description of each site or program, as well as an evaluation of strengths and weaknesses, followed by recommendations.

G. Miniproject 3

Your task is to explore the creative use of computers in your field. The types of applications may be categorized into several dimensions such as connectivity or media modality. In particular, *connectivity* refers to communications among computers: either stand-alone computers which are isolated from other machines, or networked machines which are linked to other devices on the Internet.

The *modality* refers to the nature and number of *media* used for interacting with the system. The modality pertains to both the *input* and *output* stages of an interaction with the computer.

Until the 1980s, most applications relied solely on text-based interaction: after the user types in a command through the keyboard, the software executes a fixed set of instructions, then displays the result as a string of numbers or other text. These days, user interactions usually involve multiple modes, ranging from voice input to graphic output.

The dimension of modality may be classified into the following classes.

1. Text
2. Sound
3. Images/Video
4. Graphics/Animation
5. Virtual Reality
6. Physical motion
7. Other modes

In the list above, *sound* encompasses the use of voice input from the user or speech output from the computer. On the other hand, *physical motion* includes the use of optical sensors to track the user's movements. This modality is exemplified by an input system which monitors the movements of the human eye, as when a fighter pilot selects a target for a missile by looking at a tank on the ground. *Other modes* of interaction include the monitoring of brain waves as input into a computer system, or the generation of a hologram as the output.

For each of the seven modalities above, you are to identify the most creative examples of applications in your field. Each modality should be accompanied by two digital applications: the *benchmark* program *which exists* and the best *future* application which you can *imagine*. In line with the trend toward universal access to the Internet, your futuristic program should be a networked application.

Since each of the seven modalities will yield two applications, your report will cover 14 systems. For each of the 14 programs, you are to analyze the application in terms of the nature of creativity. Examples of creative patterns include the reversal of prior assumptions, the fusion of disparate techniques, or other forms of novelty. The issues for you to consider include generic patterns of creativity, the process of innovation, and so on.

Your report should be in the form of viewgraphs: figures, tables, images, and brief passages of text. Your presentation should be packed with interesting facts and ideas, but well rehearsed for delivery within the allotted time.

H. Miniproject 4

You are to create a Website focusing on the evolution of multimedia and the Internet. The site should offer animated tutorials on historical milestones and current benchmarks relating to *technologies, tools,* and *applications.* To illustrate, the software *technology* of data compression can be employed in a *tool* such as a video distribution system, which in turn may broadcast an *application* such as a cartoon.

Hint. As a starting point for creating your Website, you should investigate online resources such as the tutorials at How Stuff Works (howstuffworks.com) or the award-winning sites linked to ThinkQuest (www.thinkquest.org).

I. Term Project 1

The term project involves the design and implementation of an *interactive tutorial* for a single user, or an *educational game.* The tutorial or game might teach players about topics such as history, art, math, science, or some other topic.

Your system "architecture" should identify all the requisite modules for your software package. Moreover, your system should implement as much of the functionality as your knowledge of Web tools permit.

The term project will serve as the integrating experience for the various topics to be addressed in this course. The project will be your masterwork, an effort which draws on the various tools and concepts you encounter in the lectures.

Requirements

Phase 1: Goals and Approach. Your proposal should do the following: (a) describe the purpose of your system, (b) conduct a benchmark survey – or identification of the best sites on the Web – for each function which pertains to your own system, (c) present the overall design of the opus you plan to create, (d) list the source(s) of content for each key module, and (e) show examples of the data, images, or other resources you expect to use.

All this information should be described in a set of slides, also known as viewgraphs. In addition, you are to submit a hardcopy of your slides. You will have several minutes to present your proposal.

The Phase 1 proposal will be an *individual* affair: each person will prepare a separate proposal. After the Phase 1 presentations, students with similar interests will form teams, each comprising several members.

Phase 2: Initial Demo. The object of this second phase is to create a preliminary version of your target software, then demonstrate how the program would appear to the user.

The presentation is to be a 2-way interaction: you will present background information while the "reviewers" in the guise of other class participants will offer suggestions and criticisms. The following topics should be covered in your presentation: system architecture (or overall layout), explanation of software modules, description of content, workplan for Phase 3, demo of preliminary software, and initial performance analysis as well as an evaluation of benchmark Web sites.

Your workplan should identify the division of responsibilities for both Phases 2 and 3: which team *member* has been assigned to what *task* for completion by which *date*. The presentation will last several minutes per team member, including time for discussion.

Phase 3: Final Results. The name of the game for the term project is quality: your approach should employ various techniques and concepts in effective ways. Your Phase 3 report should discuss key issues in design, implementation, and operation.

You will have several minutes per team member to present your term project. Your report should describe the (a) objectives, (b) methodology, (c) results, (d) evaluation of the strengths and limitations of your approach, and (e) directions for the future.

The person chiefly responsible for each particular task should prepare the documentation for that section in the form of viewgraphs. After preparing the outline of the report, each section should be assigned to a "prime author". The prime author should be clearly identified for each section of the report.

Each team may submit an optional Final Report. This report may be up to 10 pages, plus appendices consisting of exhibits such as figures, tables, an outline of your software, and a description of any other software you may have used.

Grading

The grading will be based on both the content and delivery. The content should be described in the slides you prepare for your presentation. On the other hand, the delivery refers to the professionalism in conveying interesting material to the audience for ready comprehension within a short period.

The distribution of grades among the three Phases is as follows.

Phase	Content	Delivery	Total
1	10 chips	10 chips	20 chips
2	20	20	40
3	20	20	<u>40</u>
			100 chips

Your report for Phase 3 will be graded along the following criteria.

- *Functionality:* magnitude of your objective and the effectiveness of your approach.
- *Originality:* novelty of the objective as well as your methodology.
- *Simplicity:* conceptual elegance of your approach and clarity of your report.
- *Efficiency:* minimal use of hardware and software resources, consistent with the attainment of your objective.

You need not anguish over the raw performance of your software during the operational stage. Within reason, performance attributes such as speed will not be assessed in isolation. Rather, the key to a successful term project is the effective use of the techniques and concepts discussed in class.

J. Term Project 2

Your task is to construct a Website which provides an animated guide to emerging trends and potential developments in multimedia and the Internet. In contrast to the preceding project which examines the past and present, the current exercise looks to the future. Your site should present benchmark projects in science and technology in leading laboratories around the world today, as well as their probable consequences for the future.

The theme of the Website is an international expo, with one pavilion dedicated to each of the following dates: 1, 5, 10, 20, and 50 years from now. Within each setting, you are to envisage a series of feasible scenarios for the future in terms of life at home, work, and play.

The material at the Website should be convenient to view from both full-screen devices such as desktop machines and small displays such as pocket computers. The format for this exercise is the same as the 3-phase structure for Term Project 1 in the preceding section.

Appendix F

Web Resources

The Net itself is a boundless source of information on emerging technologies and their applications in cyberspace. The resources listed below are helpful for learning, teaching, or conducting research on the past, present, and future of the digital society.

The resources are grouped by topic. Within each category, items of general scope or introductory nature are usually listed first, followed by materials of more specialized or technical focus. The selections tend to favor multimedia items over plain text or images.

Art

- *Digital Art* node under the Art Technology section at About.com: arttech.about.com
- Samples at World of Escher: *www.worldofescher.com*

Artificial Intelligence

- Keyword *Artificial Intelligence* at About Psychology: psychology.about.com

- Media linked to *Show Time* under *AI Topics* at the American Association for Artificial Intelligence: aaai.org/aitopics/html/show.html
- Slides for courses on Programming by Example at MIT: *www.media.mit.edu/people/lieber*

Artificial Life

- Keyword *Alife* at ThinkQuest: library.thinkquest.org
- Software and other items linked from Alife Online: alife.org
- Also see *Evolutionary Computation* below

Bioinformatics

- Guide to *Information Technology* at About Biotech: biotech.about.com
- Online tutorials and proceedings of the Pacific Symposium on Biocomputing: psb.stanford.edu
- Keyword *Microarray* for videos under the *Past Events* section at the National Institutes of Health: videocast.nih.gov
- Links at the European Bioinformatics Institute: *www.ebi.ac.uk*
- Also see *Biotechnology* below

Biotechnology

- Primers and *Future Directions* section at About Biotech: biotech.about.com
- Whitehead Institute at MIT: *www.wi.mit.edu*
- Overview on *Viruses* at About Biology: biology.about.com
- *Molecular Medicine* journal: muse.jhu.edu/journals/mm
- Also see *Bioinformatics* above

Business, Finance, and Economics

- Videos at *Economist*: *www.economist.tv*

- *Video Views* at *Business Week*: businessweek.com
- TV at Bloomberg: bloomberg.com
- *Watch Cnnfn Video* node at CNN-FN: *www.cnnfn.com*
- Financial News at WebFN: *www.webfn.com*
- Economics guide at About: economics.about.com
- Resources at the National Bureau of Economic Research: nber.org
- *Talks* and *Papers* at IBM Information Economies Project: *www.research.ibm.com/infoecon*
- Also see *Commerce* and *Ventures* sections below

Characters

- Items on character design at About Anime: anime.about.com

Commerce

- Ecommerce guide at About: ecommerce.about.com
- Payment schemes at PayPal: www.paypal.com
- Also see *Business, Finance, and Economics* section above

Creativity

- Keyword *Creativity* at About: about.com
- Webby Awards by the International Academy of Digital Arts and Sciences: www.iadas.net
- *Winners* node under *Interactive Entertainment* at the British Academy of Film and Television Arts: www.bafta.org
- *Studio* and other nodes at Lego: lego.com/siteindex
- Simulations and Creator tool at Stagecast: stagecast.com

Data Mining

- Guide to *Data Mining* at About Artificial Intelligence: ai.about.com

- Online text and software for WEKA (learning programs in Java) at Waikato University: www.cs.waikato.ac.nz/~ml
- Videos for keywords *Database* or *Simulation* at National Institutes of Health: videocast.nih.gov
- Clementine software at SPSS: www.spss.com
- MATLAB software for visualization at Mathworks: www.mathworks.com
- Tutorials and freeware for See5/C5.0, Cubist, and other programs at Rulequest: rulequest.com
- Statistics guide at About Math: math.about.com
- Demos and tutorials at SPSS: www.spss.com
- Demos and tutorials at SAS: www.sas.com

Education

- Prize sites at ThinkQuest: library.thinkquest.org
- *Internet Broadcasts* at Berkeley: bmrc.berkeley.edu
- Video on Demand from the University of California at San Diego: www.ucsd.tv
- *Videospace* clips at Internet2: www.internet2.edu
- Training clips at Microsoft: microsoft.com/education

Entertainment

- Goodies at Shockwave: shockwave.com
- Articles on game design at Gamespot: gamespot.com
- Visualized music at Oozic: www.oozic.com

Evolutionary Computation

- Video Lectures (#1 has webcast; others are slides) on genetic algorithms at University of Illinois: online.cen.uiuc.edu/webcourses/ge485

- Programs such as jrgp and other Java utilities from EvoNet at Napier University: evonet.napier.ac.uk
- Also see *Artificial Life* above

Future Studies

- Resources at World Future Society: wfs.org
- *Out of Control* (1995) by K. Kelly, under *Online Books* at About Artificial Intelligence: ai.about.com

Games

- Videos at Gamespot Live: live.gamespot.com
- Also see *Entertainment* above

Humor

- Items at About Humor: humor.about.com
- Humor at Monty Python: monty-python.com

Internet Studies

- *Animated Internet* at Learn the Net: learnthenet.com
- *Router* simulation at Stagecast: stagecast.com
- *Through the Wires* at ThinkQuest: library.thinkquest.org/27887
- Photo history of the Internet at the Computer History Museum Center: www.computerhistory.org/exhibits
- *How Web Pages Work* at How Stuff Works: www.howstuffworks.com
- *HTML by Example* under *Tutorials* section at Web Resources: www.nrlwebresource.com
- *Webwise* guide to the Web at BBC: www.bbc.co.uk/webwise
- Movies and tutorials at Interplanetary Internet Project: www.ipnsig.org/techinfo

Mobile Net

- *Mobile Devices* at About Portables: portables.about.com
- Dates with a virtual character, and other mobile games at Bandai: www.bandai.co.jp
- *Toolkit* from Nokia for developing wireless applications: nokia.com
- Also see *Wireless Application Protocol* below

Multimedia

- Projects at the Knowledge Management Institute of the Open University: kmi.open.ac.uk
- Projects at the MIT Media Lab: www.media.mit.edu
- Demos for Flash and Director tools at Macromedia: macromedia.com

Music

- *Software* node at About Musicians: musicians.about.com
- Music samples at MP3: mp3.com

Nanotechnology

- Links from the National Nanotechnology Initiative: nano.gov
- Online book, *Nanomedicine* (1999) by R. A. Freitas, and other links from the Foresight Institute: www.foresight.org
- Keyword *Virus* at the National Institutes of Health: videocast.nih.gov

News

- Video reports by Ananova: www.ananova.com
- Television section at CNET: www.cnettv.com
- *Interactive* node at CNN: www.cnn.tv/interactive

- Videos at Time Interactive: time.com/interactive
- Video clips at Euronews: www.euronews.net

Science

- Articles at *Scientific American* magazine: www.sciam.com
- Videos at Science and Technology News Network: www.stn2.com
- Science section at BBC Online: bbc.co.uk
- *Archive* section at *Nature Reviews*: www.nature.com/reviews
- Articles at *Science* magazine: www.sciencemag.org
- Research programs at the National Science Foundation: www.nsf.gov
- Also see *Technology* section below

Semantic Web

- *Ontology, RDF* and other items under *Semantic Web* section at W3C: w3c.org
- Tutorials on Synchronized Multimedia Integration Language at W3C: w3c.org/AudioVideo
- *SMIL Tutorial Written in SMIL*, available under the *SMIL* node at the World Wide Web Consortium (W3C): w3c.org

Streaming Video

- *Streaming video* guide at About.com: desktopvideo.about.com
- Demos and tutorials at Real Networks: www.realnetworks.com
- Channel on *Conferences* at On24: on24.com/conferences.html
- Clips at VastVideo: www.vastvideo.com
- Videos at Streaming Media: www.streamingmedia.net/video
- Videos at Windows Media: www.windowsmedia.com
- Video clips on *Streaming Video* at CyberTech Media: www.cybertechmedia.com

- Indexing methods for streaming video at Virage: www.virage.com

Technology

- News at Tech TV: techtv.com
- *Technology* node under *Video Views* at *Business Week*: businessweek.com/mediacenter
- Articles at How Stuff Works: howstuffworks.com
- Software news at Slashdot: slashdot.org
- Projects at the (Defense) Advanced Research Projects Agency: www.arpa.mil
- *Demonstrations* and *Publications* at BTexact: www.labs.bt.con/projects/ftg
- Also see *Science* section above

Ventures

- Links from Silicon Sally: siliconsally.net
- Items at About Entrepreneurs: entrepreneurs.about.com
- Section on *Venture Capital* at About Biotech: biotech.about.com
- Also see *Business, Finance and Economics* section above

Video Production

- Demos and tryout software for SnagIt, DubIt, and Camtasia (and also SDK for inserting videos into Windows applications) at TechSmith: *www.techsmith.com*
- *Hot Picks* tab at Apple Quicktime: apple.com/quicktime

Virtual Reality

- Items at About 3D Graphics: 3dgraphics.about.com

- *Product Overview* under *Product Info* for Adobe Atmosphere: www.adobe.com/products/atmosphere
- X3D for virtual reality at Web3D Consortium: web3d.org

Virus (Software)

- Digital virus guide at About: antivirus.about.com

Vocal Interaction

- Resources at VoiceXML Forum: www.voicexml.org

Wireless Application Protocol (WAP)

- Links at WAP Forum: wapforum.org
- Software development tools at WMLScript: wmlscript.com
- Also see *Mobile Net* above

References

Anand, T., et al. "KDD-95 panel on Commercial KDD Applications: The 'Secret' Ingredients for Success." www-aig.jpl.nasa.gov/kdd95/KDD95-panels.html, 1995.

Andre, E. "WIP and PPP: A Comparison of two Multimedia Presentation Systems in Terms of the Standard Reference Model." In *Computer Standards and Interfaces*, v. 18 (6-7), 1997, pp. 555-564.

Ba, S., A. B. Whinston, and H. Zhang. "Small Companies in the Digital Economy." In Brynjolfsson and Kahin (2000), pp. 185-200.

Baudin, M. "Introduction to AcknoSoft." www.acknosoft.com/#Industrial-maintenance, 1996.

Bell, D., et al. *Distributed Database Systems*. Reading, MA: Addison-Wesley, 1992.

Bigus, J. P., and J. Bigus. *Constructing Intelligent Agents with Java*. NY: Wiley Computer Publishing, 1997.

Bordegoni, M., G. Faconti, M. T. Maybury, T. Rist, S. Ruggieri, P. Trahanias, and M. Wilson. "A Standard Reference Model for Intelligent Multimedia Presentation Systems." www.dfki.de/imedia/lidos/papers/cis97, 1997.

Bourke, M. K. *Strategy and Architecture of Health Care Information Systems*. NY: Springer, 1994.

Britanik, J. and M. Marefat. "Case-Based Manufacturing Process Planning with Integrated Support for Knowledge Sharing." *Proceedings of ISATP'95*, 1995, pp. 1-14.

Brynjolfsson, E., and B. Kahin, eds. *Understanding the Digital Economy*. Cambridge, MA: MIT Press, 2000.

Brynjolfsson, E., and M. Smith. "Frictionless Commerce? A Comparison of Internet and Conventional Retailers." Working paper,

Sloan School of Management, MIT. ecommerce.mit.edu/papers/, 1999.

Business Week, Nov. 3, 1997, p. 46.

Cerf, V., S. Burleigh, A. Hooke, et al. "Interplanetary Internet (IPN): Architectural Definition." www.ipnsig.org/techinfo.htm, May 2001.

Cheeseman, P. "On Finding the Most Probable Model." In J. Shrager and P. Langley, eds., *Computational Models of Discovery and Theory Formation*, Morgan Kaufman, Palo Alto, 1990, pp. 73-96.

Chess, D., et al. "Itinerant Agent for Mobile Computing." IBM. www.cs.umbc.edu/kqml/papers/itinerant.ps, 1995.

Coen, H. M. "SodaBot: A Software Agent Construction System." MIT AI Lab. www.cs.umbc.edu/agents/papers/sodabot.ps, 1996.

Das, R., J. E. Hanson, J. O. Kephart and G. Tesauro. "Agent-Human Interactions in the Continuous Double Auction." *Proc. International Joint Conference on Artificial Intelligence*, Seattle, Aug. 2001. Also at: researchweb.watson.ibm.com/infoecon/paps/AgentHuman.pdf, 2001.

Erkes, J. W., et al. "Implementing Shared Manufacturing Services on the World-Wide Web." *Communications of the ACM*, v. 39(2), 1996: 34-45.

Etzioni, O. and D. Weld. "A Softbot-Based Interface to the Internet." *Communications of the ACM*, v. 37 (7), 1994, pp. 72-76.

Fayyad, U. M., et al. *Advances in Knowledge Discovery and Data Mining*. Cambridge, MA: AAAI / MIT Press, 1996.

Fayyad, U. M., et al. "Quest Data Mining Technologies." www.almaden.ibm.com/cs/quest/technologies.html, 1996.

Feldman, R., et al. "KDD95 Description of Demos." www-aig.jpl.nasa.gov/kdd95/KDD95-demo.html, 1996.

Finin T., et al. "A Language and Protocol to Support Intelligent Agent Interoperability." www.cs. umbc.edu/kqml/papers/cecals.ps, 1992.

Forrester Research. "Internet Commerce." www.forrester.com, 1 March 2001.

Franklin, S., et al. "Is it an Agent, or just a Program?: A Taxonomy for Autonomous Agents." Univ. of Memphis. ftp.msci.memphis.edu/comp/caat/agentprog.ps.z, 1996.

Georgia Institute of Technology. "Tenth WWW User Survey." Graphics, Visualization & Usability Center. www.gvu.gatech.edu/gvu/user_surveys, 1998.

Gershenfeld, N., and I. L. Chuang. "Quantum Computing with Molecules." *Scientific American*, v. 278, June 1998, pp. 50-55.

Gosling, J., et al. "The Java Language Environment: A Whitepaper." JavaSoft. ftp://ftp.javasoft.com/docs/whitepaper.ps.zip, 1995.

GTE. "Siftware: Tools for Data Mining and Knowledge Discovery." info.gte.com/~kdd/siftware.html, 1994.

Hardwick, M., et al. "Sharing Manufacturing Information in Virtual Enterprises." *Comm. ACM*, v. 39(2), 1996, pp. 46-54.

Hof, R. "Amazon + Wal-Mart = Win/Win." *BusinessWeek*, 2001/3/18. www.businessweek.com/bwdaily/dnflash/mar2001/nf2001038_744.htm.

Hoffman, D. L., and T. P. Novak. "Marketing in Hypermedia Computer-Mediated Environments: Conceptual Foundations." *J. of Marketing*, v. 60(3), 1996, pp. 50-68.

Hopfield, J. J. "Neural Networks and Physical Systems with Emergent Collective Computational Abilities." *Proc. Nat. Acad. Sciences USA*, v. 79(8), 1982, pp. 2554-2558.

IDC Research. "Revenues from Internet to Grow." www.idcresearch.com/ebusinesstrends/ebt20010531.stm, 21 May 2001.

Jupiter Communications. "Online Sales Increased by 54% this Holiday Season." www.jupitercommunications.com, 25 Jan. 2001.

Kim, S. H. *Essence of Creativity: A Guide to Tackling Difficult Problems.* New York: Oxford Univ. Press, 1990a.

Kim, S. H. *Designing Intelligence: A Framework for Smart Systems.* New York: Oxford Univ. Press, 1990b.

Kim, S. H. *Data Mining in Finance: Forecasting Chaotic Markets and Economies through Knowledge Discovery.* Seoul: Sigma Publishing, 1999.

Kim, S. H. "Data Mining Agents on the Wireless Internet: An Architecture and Methodology for Advanced Mobile Services." *INFORMS & KORMS Conf. Proc. 2000,* Seoul, June 2000: CD, item 4374.

Kim, S.H. and H.-H Kim. "Competitive Advantage in Cyberspace: A Comparative Analysis of Merchandising and Service Providers of Health Care". *Business Paradigms for the New Millennium: 1999 International Conf. Proc.,* Seoul, Nov. 1999: 151-9.

Kim, S.H. and J. Joo. "Enhanced Forecasting through Second-Order Learning: Case Study in Predicting Capacity Utilization". *'97 Fall Conf. Proc., Korean Institute of Industrial Engineers,* Inchon, Korea, Oct. 1997: CD, item 1-4.

Kim, S. H., O. N. Kwon, and E. J. Kim. "An Architecture for Mobile Instruction: Application to Mathematics Education through the Web." www.webmath.org/papers/mobileArchitecture, 2000.

Kim, S. H., O. N. Kwon, and E. J. Kim. "Online Mathematics: Enhancing Education through Multimedia on the Internet." www.webmath.org/papers/onlinemath, 2000.

Kim, S.H., S.W. Shin, and J. H. Kim. "Personalized Recommendations for Retailing in Internet Commerce: A Multistrategy Filtering Approach". *Proc. Int. Conf. on Electronic Commerce,* Seoul, Aug. 2000, pp. 103-111.

Kim, S.H., S. Shin, and T. Lee. "Intelligent Agents for Customized Product Design in a Virtual Shopping Mall". *Human Computer Interface '99, Spring Conf. Proc. of Korean Inf. Science Soc.,* Phoenix Park, Korea, Feb. 1999, pp. 286-293.

Kohonen, T. *Self-Organization and Associative Memory.* NY: Springer-Verlag, 1984.

Kolodner, J. L. *Case-Based Reasoning.* Morgan Kaufmann Publishers, Inc., 1993.

Korpela, E., D. Werthimer, D. Anderson, J. Cobb, and M. Lebofsky. "SETI@home: Massively Distributed Computing for SETI." *Computing in Science and Engineering*, v. 3, 2001, pp. 78-83. Also linked to SETI Website: setiathome.ssl.berkeley.edu/learnmore.html, 2001.

Koza, J. R., W. Mydlowec, G. Lanza, J. Yu, M.A. Keane. "Reverse Engineering of Metabolic Pathways from Observed Data using Genetic Programming." *Pacific Symposium on Biocomputing*, Hawaii, 2001, pp. 434-445. Also at: psb.stanford.edu/psb01.

Lee, B. H., and K. Ishii. "Product-Agents and the Embedded Web: Architecture and Tools for Lifecycle Design." dfe.stanford.edu/embedagents/aid96.html, 1996.

Lee, J. K., S. H. Kim, A. B. Whinston, and B. Schmid, eds. *Proc. of the International Conf. on Electronic Commerce.* Seoul: International Center for Electronic Commerce, 1998.

Lieberman, H. "Attaching Interface Agent Software to Applications." lieber.www.media.mit.edu/people/lieber/Lieberary/Attaching/Attaching.ps, 1996.

Lin, F., G. W. Tan, and M. J. Shaw. "Modeling Supply-Chain Networks by a Multi-Agent System." *Proc. 31st Annual Hawaii International Conference on System Sciences*, 1998.

Maes, P. "Agents that Reduce Work and Information Overload." *Communications of the ACM*, v. 37(7), 1994, pp. 31-40.

Maher, M.L. "Machine Learning in Design Expert Systems." In J. Leibowitz, ed., *Expert Systems World Congress Proceedings*, v. 1, Pergamon Press, 1991, pp. 728-736.

Mao, C., T. H. LaBean, J. H. Reif, and N. C. Seeman. "Logical Computation using Algorithmic Self-assembly of DNA Triple-crossover Molecules." *Nature*, v. 407, 2000, pp. 493-6.

236

Smart Net

McKay, P. D., et al. "An Architecture for Information Agents." www.cs.umbc.edu/kqml/papers/arpi.ps, 1996.

Minar, N., Burkhart, R., Langton, C., Askenazi, M. "The Swarm Simulation System: A Toolkit for Building Multi-Agent Simulations." www.santafe.edu/projects/swarm, 1996.

Nissen, M. "Intelligent Agents: A Technology and Business Application Analysis." haas.berkeley.edu/~heilmann/agents/index.html, 1995.

Pea, R. D., and L. M. Gomez. "Distributed Multimedia Learning Environments: Why and How?" Institute for the Learning Sciences, Northwestern U., IL, 1992.

Penrose, R. *Shadows of the Mind*. Oxford: Oxford Univ. Press, 1994.

Peterson, G. E., et al. "Using Taguchi's Method of Experimental Design to Control Errors in Layered Perceptrons." *IEEE Transactions on Neural Networks*, v. 6(4), July 1995, pp. 949-961.

Petrie, C. J. "Agent-based Engineering, the Web, and Intelligence." cdr.stanford.edu/NextLink/Expert.html, 1996.

Porter, B. W., E. R. Bareiss, and R. C. Holte. "Concept Learning and Heuristic Classification in Weak-Theory Domains." *Artificial Intelligence*, v. 45(1-2), 1990, pp. 229-63.

Porter, M. E. *Competitive Advantage*. NY: Free Press, 1985.

Porter, M. E. "Strategy and the Internet." *Harvard Business Review*, v. 79(3), 2001, pp. 62-78.

Quinlan, J. R. *C4.5: Programs for Machine Learning*. San Mateo, CA: Morgan Kaufmann, 1993.

Quinlan, J. R. "Induction of Decision Trees." *Machine Learning*, v. 1(1), 1986, pp. 81-106.

Rist, T., E. Andre, and J. Muller. "Adding Animated Presentation Agents to the Interface." *Proc. 1997 International Conference on Intelligent User Interfaces*, Orlando, Florida, 1997, pp. 79-86.

Rumelhart, D. E., G. E. Hinton, and R. J. Williams. "Learning Internal Representations by Back Propagation." In D. E. Rumelhart, J. L.

McClelland and the PDP Research Group, *Parallel Distributed Processing*, v. 1. Cambridge, MA: M.I.T. Press, 1986.

Sasisekharan, R., V. Seshadri, and S. M. Weiss. "Data Mining and Forecasting in Large-Scale Telecommunication Networks." *IEEE Expert*, February 1996, pp. 37-43.

Saxenian, A. *Regional Advantage*. Cambridge, MA: Harvard U. Press, 1996.

Schrodt, P. A., and D. J. Gerner. "Validity assessment of a machine-coded event data set for the Middle East, 1982-1992." *American Journal of Political Science*, v. 38, 1994, pp. 825-854.

Schrodt, P. A., G. D. Shannon, and J. L. Weddle. "Political Science: KEDS-A Program for the Machine Coding of Event Data." *Social Science Computer Review*, v. 12(3), 1994, pp. 561-588.

Shannon, C. E., and W. Weaver. *The Mathematical Theory of Communication*. Urbana: University of Illinois, 1949.

Shapiro, C., and H. R. Varian. *Information Rules: A Strategic Guide to the Network Economy*. Cambridge, MA: Harvard Business School Press, 1998.

Sheth, D. B. "A Learning Approach to Personalized Information Filtering." MIT, ftp://media.mit.edu/pub/agents/interface-agents/news-filter.ps, 1994.

Shoham, Y. "Agent-Oriented Programming." *Artificial Intelligence*, v. 60(1), 1993, pp. 51-92.

Silicon Graphics. "Machine Learning Library in C++." www.sgi.com/technology/mlc/docs.html, 1996.

Solis, C. R. "Virtual Worlds as Constructivist Learning Tools in a Middle School Education Environment." In B. H. Khan, ed., *Web-Based Instruction*, Englewood Cliffs, NJ: Educational Technology Publications, 1997, pp. 393-398.

Strasser, M., J. Baumann, and F. Hohl. "Mole - A Java Based Mobile Agent System." www.informatik.uni-stuttgart.de/ipvr/vs/Publications/Publications.html#1996-strasser-01, 1996.

Swami, A. "Data Mining with Silicon Graphics Technology." Silicon Graphics. www.sgi.com/software/mineset/mineset_data.html, 1995.

Sycara, K., and D. Navinchandra. "Index Transformation Techniques for Facilitating Creative Use of Multiple Cases." *Proc. 12th Int. Joint Conf. on AI*, Morgan Kaufman, Los Altos, CA, 1991, pp. 347-52.

Tsatsoulis, C., and R. L. Kashyap. "A Case-based System for Process Planning." *Robotics and Computer-Integrated Manufacturing*, v. 4(3/4), 1998, pp. 557-570.

Varian, H. R. "Market Structure in the Network Age." In E. Brynjolfsson and B. Kahin, eds., *Understanding the Digital Economy.* Cambridge, MA: MIT Press, 1999.

Vieira, J., et al. "CASTING: CAse-based reasoning: STimulation of INdustrial usaGe." MARI Computer Systems, UK, 1994.

Watson, I. "Case-Based Reasoning Development Tools: A Review." University of Salford, Bridgewater Building, Salford, UK, 1996.

Watson, I. *Applying Case-Based Reasoning Techniques for Enterprise Systems.* Los Altos, CA: Morgan Kaufmann, 1997.

Wimberley, L. "Lockheed Corporation's Recon System." hitchhiker.space.lockheed.com/~recon/data_mining.shtml, 1995.

Winfree, E., F. Liu, L. A. Wenzler, and N. C. Seeman. "Design and Self-assembly of Two-dimensional DNA Crystals." *Nature*, v. 394, 1998, pp. 539-544.

Witten, I. H., and E. Frank. *Data Mining: Practical Machine Learning Tools and Techniques with Java Implementations.* San Francisco: Morgan Kaufmann, 2000, Ch. 8.

Zdrahal, Z., and J. Domingue. "The World Wide Design Lab: An Environment for distributed Collaborative Design." In *Proc. International Conference on Engineering Design*, Tampere, Finland, August 1997. kmi.open.ac.uk/kmi-abstracts/kmi-tr-45-abstract.html.

Index

book, 12, 15-16, 18, 126, 143, 168, 212, 226
bps, 45-47
brain, 31, 123, 132, 134-135, 183, 215
branch, 36, 193
brand, 41, 83-84, 87, 89, 93, 95, 97, 107-108, 116, 168
brand identity, 84, 87, 89, 95
Brazil, 26, 56, 150
brick-and-mortar, 11
bridge, 32
broker, 58, 66
brokerage, 67, 76, 94
browser, 9, 20, 22-24, 39, 43, 74, 106, 112, 148-149, 199-200, 205, 208, 211
browsing, 105
building, 3, 121, 132, 134, 236, 238
business, 1, 3, 5, 12, 17, 29, 55, 57, 62, 68, 70-73, 84-85, 88, 91, 108, 113-114, 120, 149, 152, 162, 168, 170, 173, 181-182, 199, 210, 222-223, 228, 232, 234, 236-237
business intelligence, 1
business process reengineering, 170
business-to-business, 58, 62
buyer, 5, 62-63, 65, 74-75, 94-95, 98, 113, 116, 168
buyer power, 95, 98

byte code, 24
California, 8, 27, 41, 53, 56, 148, 153-154, 224
campaign, 82-83, 170
campus, 19
capacity utilization, 192-193, 234
car, 25, 64, 110
carbon, 130, 132-133
carbon dioxide, 130
Carebox, 96-99, 105
career, 14, 71
carnivore, 35
case, 2, 11-12, 28, 32-34, 36-38, 49, 63, 71, 74, 78-82, 84-85, 90, 101, 111, 113, 116, 118, 121, 135-136, 160, 164-165, 167, 169, 174, 178-183, 185-186, 191-193, 214, 234
case based reasoning, 12, 32-33, 37, 78-81, 113, 116, 118, 180, 182-183, 185-186, 191, 193
cash, 121, 128, 168
cat, 26
catalog, 63, 75
causal map, 102-103
caution, 84
CBR, 32-33, 78, 81-82, 116, 185-186, 191-195
cell, 37-38, 132, 134
cellar, 137
cellphone, 29
cellular phone, 46

Department of Defense, 4, 8

design, 14-15, 29, 32-33, 35-36, 42,
53, 55, 71, 73, 87, 93, 113-117,
161, 167, 174, 178, 181, 185-
186, 188, 210-211, 214, 216-
218, 223-224, 234-236, 238

destination, 19, 130, 146

destiny, 14

diagnostic, 48

dialogue, 42, 51, 130

diet, 35

differentiation, 93-94

digital divide, 69, 84

Digital Equipment Corporation,
54

digital rights management, 66

Digital Subscriber Line, 45

digitopia, 5, 7, 11, 13, 58, 67, 73,
96, 110, 122-124

dirtspace, 83

discovery, 15, 29-31, 40, 77, 86,
181, 232-234

distance learning, 27

Distributed Terascale Facility, 47

distribution, 13, 59, 61, 64, 73-74,
76, 78, 89, 93-94, 97, 99, 106,
108, 114, 147, 216, 218

diversification, 82

diversity, 93, 104, 160, 177

DNS, 21

doctor, 14

dog, 26, 50, 174

domain, 20-21, 32, 35, 40, 53, 63,
74, 76, 114, 118, 128, 188

domain name, 20-21, 63

Domain Name Server, 21

Download.com, 59

driving, 88, 138

drugs, 96-98

DSL, 45

dustville, 105, 122

dynamic pricing, 73

dystopia, 123

E*Offering, 66

Earth, 13, 20, 48-49, 130-131, 137

East Coast, 54

eBay, 58, 62

ecommerce, 73, 88, 96, 223, 232

economic growth, 5, 7, 33, 37, 68,
89, 107, 164

economy, 2, 12, 15, 37, 42, 52-53,
55, 64, 67, 69-70, 73, 87, 92, 122,
231, 237-238

education, 8, 14-15, 46, 52, 165,
173-179, 190, 211, 224, 234, 237

effectiveness, 2, 37, 43, 50, 124,
156, 162, 198, 213, 219

efficacy, 104, 160, 168, 182

efficiency, 2, 5, 43, 71, 91, 104, 107,
115, 124, 157, 162, 166, 212-
213, 219

effort, 7, 30, 59, 77, 131, 160, 167,
217

EIS, 119-120, 169

microtubule, 132
migration, 60, 96
Milky Way Galaxy, 49
millennium, 0-1, 13, 27, 44, 48, 53, 72, 92, 107, 109-110, 117, 123, 127, 134, 137, 175, 179, 234
MIME, 21
mind, 111, 120, 126, 132, 136, 168, 236
mission, 48, 56, 68, 72, 98, 100, 137, 139, 160, 179
mission control, 48
MIT, 23, 54, 141, 201, 222, 226, 231-232, 235, 237-238
mobile media, 44, 111, 153
mobility, 85, 184
model, 26, 31, 41, 61-63, 81, 87, 89, 101, 107, 115, 127, 150, 184, 186, 188, 193, 195, 199, 231-232
money, 11, 29, 199
monitor, 17, 30, 74, 77, 125, 129, 138, 188
Moon, 130, 138
mortician, 14
MOSWT diagram, 100-101
motion, 24, 144, 215
motivation, 77, 144, 152
mouse, 5, 43, 84, 200, 206, 208
movie, 23, 25, 46, 154
MP3, 105, 226
multichannel marketing, 76
multichannel retailing, 76

multimedia, 1, 3, 6, 12, 15, 22, 24-25, 43, 45-47, 49-51, 71-72, 74, 85, 111, 113, 119, 143-144, 146, 151, 156-157, 159, 164, 166, 174, 178, 180, 186-188, 201-204, 213, 216, 219, 221, 226-227, 231, 234, 236
Multipart Internet Mail Encoding, 21
multiple regression, 79-80, 86
multistrategy approach, 37, 191
municipality, 17
music, 28, 39, 45, 47, 64-65, 127, 138, 150, 179, 224, 226
mutation, 34-35
name, 4, 20-21, 28, 47, 63, 84, 167, 192, 211, 218
nanotechnology, 98, 133, 226
National Transportation Exchange, 58
natural language, 27, 41, 111, 117, 119, 153
natural language processing, 41, 117
navigation, 74, 86
Navigator, 22, 205, 208, 211
Nazi, 7
necessity, 15, 129
neighborhood, 8, 17, 52, 61
Net, 1-6, 8-14, 16, 18, 20, 22-28, 30-32, 34, 36, 38, 40, 42-50, 54, 56-64, 66-68, 72, 74-76, 78-80,

opportunities, 57, 66-67, 92, 98, 100, 113, 164

optimism, 80

optimization, 34, 78

order, 11, 19-20, 24, 59, 64, 74-75, 83, 85-86, 97-98, 129, 199-200

ordering, 105, 154

organization, 2, 4, 12, 17, 49, 53, 58, 60, 82, 98-100, 102, 104, 120, 159-160, 163, 165-167, 170

Oslo, 182

Outblaze, 60

outer space, 18, 130-131

output, 31, 37, 42, 52, 65, 80, 191-193, 195, 214-215

outsourcing, 71, 100, 166-167

owner, 26, 35, 59, 65, 107, 114, 120, 135

pacemaker, 135

Palo Alto Research Center, 41

panorama, 57, 137

paradigm, 76, 114

Paradox, 57

parallel, 1, 10, 24, 34, 36, 70, 76, 117, 134, 236-237

paralysis, 72

parent, 41, 129

park, 26, 234

participant, 24, 211

particle, 131, 133, 136

partnership, 83, 85

PC, 27, 65-66, 106-107, 117, 160, 206, 208-209

peasant, 14

Penrose Roger, 132, 236

performance, 25, 79-80, 94, 104, 114-116, 127-128, 139, 181-184, 195-196, 217, 219

persistence, 121, 156

personal computer, 27, 64, 114-115

personality, 6, 26, 77, 167

Personalized Plan-based Presenter, 188

personnel, 98, 164-165

pessimism, 80

pet, 26, 121

phenotype, 34

Philippines, 55

phone, 5, 20, 45-46, 64, 75, 95

phone bill, 64

phospholipid cycle, 127

physicist, 132

physiological process, 127

pilgrimage, 12

pizza, 63

plan, 67, 88, 162, 164, 169, 171, 217

planet, 1, 11, 18-19, 28-29, 44, 48-49, 53, 59, 82, 85, 121, 130

planning, 10, 29, 33, 53, 74, 78, 89-90, 92, 115, 152, 160, 164, 166-167, 190, 231, 238

programming language, 28, 49, 174

promise, 3, 29, 89, 123, 159, 173-174

promotion, 76, 97

property, 22, 31, 64, 121, 131, 156

prosperity, 52, 69, 168

prosthetic, 135

protein computation, 134

prototype, 8-9, 32, 39, 115

proxy, 128

psychographics, 77

public, 21, 48, 54, 66, 80, 104, 117, 168, 174

PublishOne, 65

punishment, 137

purchasing, 62, 77, 79-80, 105

quality, 2, 93, 99, 104, 113, 218

quantum coherence, 133

quantum computing, 133, 233

quantum mechanics, 132

Quicken, 39

radiation, 135

radio, 61, 78

Radiolinja, 64

RAND, 8

raw data, 50, 86, 114, 159

reach, 13, 18, 21, 34-35, 57-58, 72, 85, 108, 131, 136, 157, 162

real world, 26, 30, 80, 120, 122-123, 127, 147

realspace, 26, 81, 84-85, 90, 96, 107-108, 122-123

recruiting, 75

regression, 30, 79-81, 86

regulation, 97, 99, 134

reliability, 10, 19, 97, 161

religion, 11, 60

rental, 60-62

reputation, 89, 99, 104-105

research, 8-9, 13, 30, 41, 46-47, 53-55, 59, 100, 120, 127, 141, 180, 201, 204, 221, 223, 227-228, 232-233, 236-237

researcher, 129

responsiveness, 17, 104-105, 129, 166, 184

restructuring, 3, 91-92

retail, 57, 59, 62, 73-74, 95

return on investment, 4

revenue, 60, 63, 92, 203

revenue models, 60, 92

revolution, 0-1, 3, 18, 51, 67

risk, 33, 60, 90-91, 98, 117-119, 163-164, 168

risk assessment, 117, 119

Rite Aid, 98

rival, 11, 105

rivalry, 93, 96, 99

robustness, 31, 79, 145, 185, 190

rockspace, 82, 90, 108

Route 128, 53-54

router, 21, 146, 225

sleep, 121
smart software, 12, 50, 76, 85-86, 110, 114, 181
SMIME, 21
SMTP, 21, 145
socializing, 27
societal welfare, 72
society, 5, 12, 15, 17-18, 21, 48, 53, 59, 68, 111, 125-126, 129, 138, 141, 190, 221, 225
Softbank Corporation, 66
software, 2-6, 9-10, 12, 15, 18, 20, 22, 24-27, 29-32, 38-39, 41-42, 46-48, 50, 55-56, 59-63, 65-66, 70, 74, 76-77, 84-86, 91, 94, 99-100, 106-108, 110-112, 114-115, 118-119, 121, 126-128, 139, 145, 148-149, 152, 161, 170, 175, 177-178, 180-181, 185-186, 200-202, 204-206, 208-209, 214-219, 222, 224, 226, 228-229, 232, 235, 238
solar system, 18, 48, 131
soldier, 129
Son Masayoshi*****
song, 65, 105
Sony Communication Network, 26
sound, 3, 24-25, 130, 144, 147, 215
Soviet Union, 8, 52

space, 1, 12, 18, 26, 48-49, 58, 91, 94, 105, 120-121, 124, 130-131, 156, 180, 184, 238
spacecraft, 13, 48-49, 131, 137
spatial reasoning, 178
special effects, 6, 46
specs, 114, 116
spectator, 173
spectrum, 12, 33, 47, 87, 90, 138
speculative bubble, 67, 92
speed, 1, 5, 17, 29, 44-46, 56, 87, 91, 97, 105-106, 125, 131, 135, 170, 185, 219
stability, 35, 178
standard, 11, 19, 21-23, 27-28, 41, 44, 48-49, 55, 64, 68, 79, 88, 90, 112, 127, 131, 146-147, 149, 154-155, 162, 174, 231
standard of living, 68
Stanford University, 9, 54
statistics, 29-30, 37, 50, 78, 80, 86, 182, 224
status, 11, 20, 61, 92, 110, 146
stock market, 29-30, 66, 190
stocks, 29, 32, 36, 127
store, 41, 59, 83-84
story telling, 33
strategist, 86-87
strategy, 13-14, 41, 68, 87, 91, 96, 99, 102-103, 105, 107-109, 159-160, 162, 164, 167, 171, 210, 231, 236

131, 134, 137, 139, 156, 159-
160, 168, 182, 184, 193, 216,
218, 222, 227
time to market, 71
timeliness, 71, 105-106, 131
Tomlinson Ray, 9
tortoise, 26
toy, 6, 83-84
Toyota, 68
Toys R Us, 83
trade, 17-18, 49, 66-67, 85, 122,
156
tradition, 19, 58, 145, 163
traffic, 19, 63, 110, 153, 186
transaction, 5, 58-60, 62-63, 95,
106, 127, 138
transaction processing, 106
transition, 89, 136
Transmission Control Protocol, 9,
130
Transport Control Protocol, 19
travel, 5-6, 18, 52, 58, 71, 75, 105,
198, 210
travel industry, 5
travel time, 71
Travelers Group, 71
tree, 36, 193-194
trust, 84, 184
tsunami, 5
tune, 23, 62, 180
tunneling, 131-132
turmoil, 109-110, 168

tutorial, 13, 143, 209, 216, 227
Ultra system, 7
uncertainty, 90-91
Uniform Resource Locator, 22-23,
150
United States, 7, 14, 40, 53, 62
universe, 133, 137
University of Washington, 39
Unix, 20, 160
upheaval, 49
URL, 22-23, 146, 150, 199-200
usability, 106, 233
usage, 40, 65, 77, 79, 97, 238
user, 1-2, 6, 12, 20, 24-26, 29, 31-
32, 37, 43-46, 52-53, 57, 59, 61,
74, 80, 85, 104, 106, 110-111,
113-117, 120, 144, 146-147,
151-152, 157, 166, 169, 173,
175, 178, 180, 183-189, 213-
217, 233, 236
Utah, 8
utility, 18, 39, 63, 81-82, 97, 177-
178, 192, 206
utopia, 123
vacuum tube, 7-8
value, 11, 34, 67, 77, 81, 84-85,
107-108, 121, 156, 183, 193
value-added services, 64, 67
vassal, 14
veggies, 35
vehicle, 1, 21, 40, 49, 59, 62, 64-66,
68, 76, 180, 186

Notes

Chapter 1

[1] *The Economist*, 7/26/99, p. S-22.

Chapter 2

[2] Kim, 1994b; Nissen, 1995.

[3] Fayyad et al., 1996; Wimberley, 1995.

[4] Kim, 1992; etc.

[5] Rumelhart et al., 1986.

[6] Goldberg, 1989; Holland, 1975.

[7] Quinlan, 1986.

[8] Kim, 1999.

[9] Anand, 1995; Baudin, 1996; GTE, 1994; Kim, 1999; Quinlan, 1986, 1993; Silicon Graphics, 1996; Swami, 1995; Vieira et al., 1994; Watson, 1996; Wimberley, 1995; Witten and Frank, 2000.

[10] The homepage of the Internet 2 consortium is *www.internet2.edu.*

[11] *A floating point* is the digital format used by a computer to represent a real number such as "3.7". For an arithmetic operation such as addition or division, grappling with floating point data is more cumbersome and takes longer than working with integers such as "4" or "-17". Since technical calculations usually require floating points, however, a supercomputer is rated by its ability to crunch such data. One *floating* point *op*eration (*flop*) per *second* is known as a *flops*. A trillion flops then comprise a *teraflops*.

[12] Korpela et al., 2001.

[13] The Interplanetary Internet Project is a special interest group within the Internet Society. The latter organization monitors new developments in technology and applications, then promotes changes in Internet standards. The Website for the Internet Society is *www.isoc.org*; that for the Interplanetary Project is *www.ipnsig.org*.

Chapter 3

[14] Saxenian, 1996.
[15] *Business Week*, 2000/2/7, p. EB-16.
[16] *The Economist*, 1999/7/26, p. S-21.
[17] Goldman Sachs, 1999.

Chapter 4

[18] IDC, 2001.
[19] Jupiter, 2001.
[20] Forrester, 2001.
[21] Fayyad, 1996; Wimberley, 1995.
[22] Hopfield, 1982; etc.
[23] Kim, 1994; etc.
[24] Kim, 1992; etc.
[25] Georgia, 1998.
[26] Kim and Min, 1999.
[27] Kim and Min, 1999.
[28] Hof, 2001.
[29] Brynjolfsson and Smith, 1999.
[30] Boston, 1999.

Chapter 5

[31] Ba et al., 2000.
[32] Porter, 1985.
[33] Bourke, 1994, p. 30.
[34] Kim and Kim, 1999.
[35] Porter, 2001.

Chapter 6

[36] Kim, 1999.
[37] Kim et al., 1999, 2000.
[38] Kohonen, 1984.
[39] Schrodt and Gerner, 1984; Schrodt et al., 1994.
[40] Kim, 1999.
[41] One line of development is described in Kim (2000).

Chapter 7

[42] At the end of the 120th generation, the best individual from the genetic population identified the correct topology for the chemical pathways. The rate for each reaction, however, was still incorrect. This shortcoming was rectified by the 225th generation. At this juncture, the best individual embodied the proper topology as well as presentable reaction rates: out of four reactions, one was accurate to within 2% of the correct rate, and the others to three significant digits (Koza et al., 2001).

[43] Das et al., 2001.
[44] Cerf et al., 2001.
[45] Penrose, 1994, p. 372.
[46] Both types of atoms also contain neutrons, but the latter are electrically neutral. They play no part in chemical reactions or

compound effects such as the bonds of attraction which keep a protein molecule intact.

[47] Gershenfeld and Chuang, 1998.

[48] Mao et al., 2000; Winfree et al., 1998.

Appendix B

[49] Kim, 1990a, p. 53.

Appendix C

[50] Pea and Gomez, 1992.

[51] Solis, 1997.

[52] Bordegoni et al., 1997.

[53] Andre, 1997.

Appendix D

[54] Kim, 1994a.

[55] Shoham, 1993.

[56] Maes, 1994.

[57] Etzioni and Weld, 1994.

[58] Lieberman, 1996.

[59] Coen, 1996.

[60] Franklin, 1996.

[61] Sheth, 1994.

[62] Chess, 1995.

[63] Bell, 1992.

[64] Finin, 1992; McKay, 1996.

[65] Gosling, 1995, 1996a, 1996b.

[66] Kim, 1990b.

[67] Zdrahal and Domingue, 1997.

68 Bordegoni et al., 1997.
69 Rist et al., 1997.
70 Hopfield, 1982; etc.
71 Kim, 1994a, 1994b.
72 Kim, 1999; Kim and Novick, 1993.
73 Quinlan, 1986.
74 Kim and Joo, 1997.

0-595-21382-0

www.ingramcontent.com/pod-product-compliance
Lightning Source LLC
Chambersburg PA
CBHW051226050326
40689CB00007B/815